The
Black
Student's
Guide
to
Scholarships

The
Black
Student's
Guide
to
Scholarships

600+ Private Money Sources
for Black and Minority Students

Fourth Edition

Edited by Barry Beckham

Edmond Chang, Databasing and Typesetting
Anika Simmons, Summer Intern, Howard University

MADISON BOOKS
Lanham • New York • London

Published by Madison Books
4501 Forbes Boulevard, Suite 200, Lanham, Maryland 20706
http://www.rlpgtrade.com

10 Thornbury Road, Plymouth PL6 7PP, United Kingdom

Distributed by National Book Network

British Library Cataloguing in Publication Information Available

Library of Congress Cataloging-in-Publication Data Available

ISBN 13: 978-1-56833-079-2 pbk: alk. paper)

♾™ The paper used in this publication meets the minimum requirements of American National Standard for Information Sciences—Permanence of Paper for Printed Library Materials, ANSI/NISO Z39.48-1992.

Printed in the United States of America

CONTENTS

MESSAGE TO THE BLACK STUDENT

I know, you want to get started looking for money. You're ready to get paid, and you hope this introduction is short enough so you can get down to business. Okay, I'll try to make it as short as I can.

Far too many black students don't go to college because they think they can't afford it. Nothing could be farther from the truth. There is plenty of money available for you! The issue is really one of information. Information is power, and if you have access to it, you have access to the tools to accomplish your goals.

There are approximately 150 books available that list financial aid opportunities for various academic activities. If you don't know about some of these publications, you are even farther away from the information you need. Here then is the revised edition of a guide that began as a pamphlet listing 75 scholarships for black students. The more I read, and the more I researched, the more I discovered. Now the guide lists more than 650 sources.

Anyone who can read can collect this information. I have a favorite answer to questions that I am asked on a regular basis from students, parents and others. "Where do I find the information?" they ask. Okay, here is the little-known secret: GO TO THE LIBRARY. Ask the librarian to point you in the direction of the information you seek, whether it is about financial aid, summer employment, foreign study, publishing a book or the phone number of a famous athlete.

It's that simple—as simple as the response Bill Cosby gives when people ask him how he and Camille have stayed married so long. "Go home," is his answer.

You go too—to the library—and ask.

And while we're on the subject of asking, don't be afraid to ask the people who get paid to help you—the financial aid officers at colleges in America. Tell them you're serious about your education which is the key to your future and the future of black American, and you want information, answers to your questions. They are supposed to help you, and they should have answers to all the questions listed at the end of the section on federal loans. Stand up for your rights and ask for the information. Information is power. And like power, it's usually not just given to you.

On the subject of loans, I get confused. Black parents are sometimes so uptight about borrowing money for their children's future. It's as if it is not one of the most important investments they can make, the return on which is incalculable. Actually, you can calculate it. The Census Department has already found that a male with a college degree will earn about a million dollars more in his lifetime than a male without a degree. But those same parents have no qualms about purchasing a new car, new jewelry, new clothing—consumables that have little lifetime value. Loans are not the worst case scenario, particularly if you can find one of the new programs that combine elements like savings, life insurance and consolidation of several obligations. And of course you want to borrow as little as possible and be aware of the stiff penalties involved if you miss payments. Finally, though, how can you walk away from your future because you don't want to invest in it?

Please note that the scholarships offered by educational institutions can not be used at other schools. So don't write to Stanford expecting to use their scholarship at Morehouse. Many college officials have asked me to make this policy clear because they are bombarded by misguided applications from students who say they got the information from this guide.

Send your request on a postcard and save money. You can purchase 50 for 20 cents each for a total of $10.00 rather than spend $16.00 for the same number of 32 cents stamps plus more money for envelopes and stationery. You will write: Dear Sir or Madam, Please send information and application forms for the [name of the scholarship] to [your name and address]. Thank you for your cooperation. Sign it, put a reminder in your scholarship notebook (which includes all information about scholarships you have collected), and mail it off. You're in the running! Look out Michael Johnson.

If you have additions, questions or need to contact me, please write via postal service or e-mail (beckham@erols.com). Your future is inextricably linked to your educational attainment. Therefore, the future of black American is linked to your progress because you are our future. To emphasize this last point, I want you to know that when I asked Bill Cosby for permission to use his photograph on the cover of this book, he responded within two weeks. He knows how important you are.

Barry Beckham
July 1996
P.O.Box 8008
Silver Spring, MD 20907

FINANCIAL AID PROGRAMS FROM THE U.S. DEPARTMENT OF EDUCATION

A. WHERE TO FIND OUT ABOUT STUDENT AID

1. The financial aid administrator (FAA) at each school in which you're interested can tell you what aid programs are available there and how much the total cost of attendance will be.

2. The state higher education agency in your home state can give you information about state aid including aid from the State Student Incentive Grant (SSIG) Program, which is jointly funded by individual states and the U.S. Department of Education.

3. The agency in your state responsible for public elementary and secondary schools can give you information on the Robert C. Byrd Honors Scholarship Program (Byrd Program). To qualify for aid under the Byrd Program, you must demonstrate outstanding academic achievement and show promise of continued academic excellence.

   For the address and telephone number of the appropriate state agency, contact your school's financial aid office or call: 1-800-4-FED-AID (1-800-433-3243).

4. The AmeriCorps program provides full-time educational awards in return for work in community service. You can work before, during, or after your postsecondary education, and you can use the funds either to pay current educational expenses or to repay federal student loans. For more information on this program, call: 1-800-942-2677 or write to: The Corporation for National and Community Service, 1201 New York Avenue, NW, Washington, DC 20525.

5. Your public library is an excellent source of information on state and private sources of aid.

6. Many companies, as well as labor unions, have programs to help pay the cost of postsecondary education for employees, members, or their children.

7. Check foundations, religious organizations, fraternities or sororities, and town or city clubs. Include community organizations and civic groups such as the American Legion, YMCA, 4-H Club, Elks, Kiwanis, Jaycees, Chamber of Commerce, and the Girl or Boy Scouts.

8. Don't overlook aid from organizations connected with your field of interest (for example, the American Medical Association or the American Bar Association). These organizations are listed in the U.S. Department of Labor's *Occupational Outlook Handbook* and are also listed in various directories of associations available at your public library.

9. If you (or your spouse) are a veteran or the dependent of a veteran, veterans educational benefits may be available. Check with your local Veterans' Affairs office.

B. THE U.S. DEPARTMENT OF EDUCATION STUDENT FINANCIAL AID (SFA) PROGRAMS

I.   Federal Pell Grants
II.   Federal Stafford Loans
III. Federal PLUS Loans
IV.   Federal Consolidation Loans
V.   Federal Supplemental Educational Opportunity Grants (FSEOG)
VI.   Federal Work-Study (FWS)
VII. Federal Perkins Loans

REMEMBER THESE KEY DEFINITIONS

Grants are financial aid you don't have to pay back.
Work-Study lets you work and earn money to help pay for school.
Loans are borrowed money that you must repay with interest.
Undergraduates may receive all three types of financial aid. Graduate students may receive loans or Federal Work-Study, but not Federal Pell Grants or FSEOG. Not all schools take part in all the programs. To find out which ones are available at a particular school, contact the financial aid office.

STUDENT ELIGIBILITY

To receive aid from the major student aid programs, you must:

1. Have financial need, except for some loan programs (see below).

2. Have a high school diploma or a General Education Development (GED) Certificate, pass a test approved by the U.S. Department of Education, or meet other standards your state establishes that are approved by the U.S. Department of Education. See your financial aid administrator for more information.

3. Be enrolled or accepted for enrollment as a regular student working toward a degree or certificate in an eligible program. (You may not receive aid for correspondence or telecommunications courses unless they are part of an associate, bachelor's, or graduate degree program.)

4. Be a U.S. citizen or eligible noncitizen.

5. Have a valid Social Security Number.

6. Make satisfactory academic progress.

7. Sign a statement of educational purpose and a certification statement on overpayment and default (both found on the Free Application for Federal Student Aid (FAFSA)).

8. Register with the Selective Service, if required.

FINANCIAL NEED

Aid from most of the major government programs is awarded on the basis of financial need (except for subsidized Stafford, all PLUS and Consolidation loans).

When you apply for federal student aid, the information you report is used in a formula, established by the U.S. Congress, that calculates your Expected Family Contribution (EFC), an amount you and your family are expected to contribute toward your education. If your EFC is below a certain amount, you'll be eligible for a Federal Pell Grant, assuming you meet all other eligibility requirements.

There isn't a maximum EFC that defines eligibility for the other financial aid programs. Instead, your EFC is used in an equation to determine your financial need:

> Cost of attendance
> − <u>Expected Financial Contribution (EFC)</u>
> = Financial Need

Your financial aid administrator (FAA) calculates your cost of attendance (COA) and subtracts the amount you and your family are expected to contribute toward that cost. If there's anything left over, you're considered to have financial need. In determining your need for aid from the SFA programs, your FAA must first consider other aid you're expected to receive.

Your FAA can adjust the EFC formula's data elements or adjust your COA if he or she believes your family's financial circumstances warrant it based on the documentation you provide. However, the FAA does not have to make such an adjustment. See Special Circumstances for more information.

You can get a booklet called the "Expected Family Contribution (EFC) Formulas," which describes how the EFC formulas are calculated, by writing to:

Federal Student Aid Information Center
P.O. Box 84
Washington, DC 20044

I. FEDERAL PELL GRANTS

What Is a Federal Pell Grant?

A Federal Pell Grant, unlike a loan, does not have to be repaid. Pell Grants are awarded only to undergraduate students who have not earned a bachelor's or professional degree. (A professional degree would be a degree in a field such as pharmacy or dentistry.) For many students, Pell Grants provide a foundation of financial aid to which other aid may be added.

How Do I Qualify?

To determine if you're eligible financially, the U.S. Department of Education uses a standard formula, established by Congress, to evaluate the information you report when you apply. The formula produces an Expected Family Contribution (EFC) number. Your Student Aid Report (SAR) contains this number and will tell you if you're eligible.

How Much Money Can I Get?

Awards for the 1996-97 award year (July 1, 1996 to June 30, 1997) will have a maximum amount of $2,470. You can receive only one Pell Grant in an award year. How much you get will depend not only on your EFC, but also on your cost of attendance, whether you're a full-time or part-time student, and whether you attend school for a full academic year or less. You may not receive Pell Grant funds from more than one school at a time.

II. FEDERAL STAFFORD LOANS

Stafford Loans are either subsidized or unsubsidized. A subsidized loan is awarded on the basis of financial need. The federal government pays interest on the loan ("subsidizes" the loan) until you begin repayment and during authorized periods of deferment.

An unsubsidized loan is not awarded on the basis of need. You'll be charged interest from the time the loan is disbursed until it is paid in full. If you allow the interest to accumulate, it will be capitalized—that is, the interest will be added to the principal amount of your loan and will increase the amount you have to repay. If you choose to pay the interest as it accumulates, you'll repay less in the long run.

You can receive a subsidized Stafford Loan and an unsubsidized Stafford Loan for the same enrollment period.

Who Can Get a Stafford Loan?

If you're a regular student enrolled in an eligible program of study at least half time, you may receive a Stafford Loan. You must also meet other general eligibility requirements.

How Much Can I Borrow?

If you're a dependent undergraduate student, you can borrow up to these amounts:

— $2,625 if you're a first-year student enrolled in a program of study that is at least a full academic year;

— $3,500 if you've completed your first year of study, and the remainder of your program is at least a full academic year; or

— $5,500 a year if you've completed two years of study, and the remainder of your program is at least a full academic year.

If you're an independent undergraduate student or a dependent student whose parents are unable to get a PLUS Loan, you can borrow up to these amounts:

— $6,625 if you're a first-year student enrolled in a program of study that is at least a full academic year (at least $4,000 of this amount must be in unsubsidized loans);

— $7,500 if you've completed your first year of study, and the remainder of your program is at least a full academic year (at least $4,000 of this amount must be in unsubsidized loans); or

— $10,000 a year if you've completed two years of study, and the remainder of your program is at least a full academic year (at least $5,000 of this amount must be in unsubsidized loans).

If you're a graduate student, you can borrow up to $18,500 each academic year (at least $10,000 of this amount must be in unsubsidized Stafford loans).

The total debt you can have outstanding from all Stafford Loans combined is:

— $23,000 as a dependent undergraduate student;

— $46,000 as an independent undergraduate student (no more than $23,000 of this amount may be in subsidized loans); or

— $138,500 as a graduate or professional student (no more than $65,000 of this amount may be in subsidized loans). The graduate debt limit includes any Stafford Loans for undergraduate study.

What's the Interest Rate Charged on These Loans?

If you have a Stafford Loan that was first disbursed on or after July 1, 1994, the interest rate could change each year of repayment, but it will never exceeded 8.25 percent. The interest rate is adjusted each year on

July 1. You'll be notified of interest rate changes throughout the life of your loan.

DIRECT STAFFORD LOANS

How Do I Apply for a Direct Stafford Loan?

First, complete the 1996-97 Free Application for Federal Student Aid (FAFSA) or Renewal FAFSA. After your FAFSA is processed, your school will review the results and will inform you of your loan eligibility.

Second, complete the promissory note provided by your school or the Direct Loan Servicing Center. Remember, the promissory note is a legal document requiring you to repay the loan. Read it carefully before you sign.

Loan payments are made to the U.S. Department of Education. For more information on repayment options, write for a copy of the Direct Loans Repayment Book at the following address:

Federal Student Aid Information Center
P.O. Box 84
Washington, DC 20044

FFEL STAFFORD LOANS

How Do I Apply for a FFEL Stafford Loan?

First, complete the 1996-97 Free Application for Federal Student Aid (FAFSA) or Renewal FAFSA. After your FAFSA is processed, your school will review the results and will inform you of your loan eligibility.

Second, complete the Federal Stafford Loan Application and promissory note available from your school, a lender, or your state guaranty agency. Remember, the promissory note is a legal document requiring you to repay the loan. Read it carefully before you sign.

Third, take your completed Federal Stafford Loan Application and Promissory Note to the school you plan to attend. After the school completes its portion of the application, you (or the school on your behalf) must send the application to a lender for evaluation.

How Can I Find a Lender?

Contact the guaranty agency that serves your state. For your agency's address and telephone number, and for more information about borrowing, call the Federal Student Aid Information Center's toll-free number: 1-800-4-FED-AID (1-800-4-33-3243).

OTHER SOURCES:

AMS Education Loan Trust: 1-800-637-3060

Bank of America Loan Center: 1-800-344-8382

Bank One, Indiana, N.A.: 1-800-288-6144

National College Funding Services, Inc., has developed an innovative college assistance program which includes a savings plan. Unlike many banks and groups which earn huge profits on loan interest and collection fees, NCFS sells its loans immediately to Sallie Mae. Contact Ivor Holmquist, NCFS, 7534 Ritchie Highway, Suite 5, Glen Burnie, MD 21061 or telephone (410) 321-1864 or (410) 761-0790.

University Support Services, Inc., offers a PLATO student loan program with $25,000 yearly maximums and a consolidation program lowering monthly loan payments up to 35 percent using a 20-year repayment period: 1-800-230-4080 or email: ussinfo@aol.com.

USA Group issues, guarantees, and services educational loans: 1-800-LOAN-USA or email: loanapps@usagroup.com.

III. PLUS LOANS (LOANS FOR PARENTS)

Federal PLUS Loans (PLUS Loans) enable parents with good credit histories to borrow to pay the educational expenses of each child who is a dependent undergraduate student enrolled at least half time. PLUS Loans are available through both the Direct Loan and FFEL programs. Most of the benefits to parent borrowers are identical in the two programs.

Are There Any Borrowing Requirements My Parents Have to Meet?

Yes. To be eligible to receive a PLUS Loan, your parents generally will be required to pass a credit check. If they don't pass the credit check, they might still be able to receive a loan if someone, such as a relative or friend who is able to pass the credit check, agrees to endorse the loan, promising to repay it if your parents should fail to do so. Your parents might also qualify for a loan even if they don't pass the credit check if they can demonstrate that extenuating circumstances exist. You must meet the general eligibility requirements for federal student financial aid. Your parents must also meet some of these general requirements. For example, your parents must meet citizenship requirements and may not be in default or owe a refund to any SFA programs.

How Much Can My Parents Borrow?

The yearly limit on either type of PLUS Loan is equal to your cost of attendance minus any other financial aid you receive. For example, if your cost of attendance is $6,000 and your receive $4,000 in other financial aid, your parents could borrow up to—but no more than—$2,000.

What's the Interest Rate on PLUS Loans?

The interest rate is variable, but it will never exceed 9 percent. The interest rate is adjusted each year on July 1. Your parents will be notified of interest rate changes throughout the life of their loan(s). Interest is charged on the loan from the date the first disbursement is made until the loan is paid in full.

Do My Parents Need to Find a Lender?

No. Under the Direct Loan Program, their lender will be the U.S. Department of Education. Your school assists the federal government in administering the Direct Loan Program by distributing the loan application, processing the loan, and delivering the loan funds.

FFEL PLUS LOANS

How Do My Parents Apply for an FFEL PLUS Loan?

Your parents must submit a completed PLUS Loan Application (available from your school, a lender, or your state guaranty agency) to your school. After the school completes its portion of the application, it must be sent to a lender for evaluation. Because your financial need does not have to be evaluated, you do not need to file a FAFSA, unless your school requires it.

How Can My Parents Find a Lender?

Your parents should contact the guaranty agency that serves your state. For your agency's address and telephone number, and for more information about borrowing, call the Federal Student Aid Information Center's toll-free number: 1-800-4-FED-AID (1-800-4-33-3243).

IV. CONSOLIDATION LOANS

Consolidation Loans allow a borrower to combine different types of federal student loans to simplify repayment. (A borrower with just one loan can also choose to consolidate it.) Both the Direct Loan Program and the FFEL Program offer consolidation loans. However, Direct Consolidation Loans and FFEL Consolidation Loans are very different and are discussed separately here.

DIRECT CONSOLIDATION LOANS

A Direct Consolidation Loan is designed to help student and parent borrowers simplify loan repayment. Even though you might have several different federal student loans, you'll make only one payment a month for all the loans you consolidate. You can even consolidate just one loan into a Direct Consolidation Loan to get benefits such as flexible repayment options.

What Kinds of Loans Can Be Consolidated Under a
Direct Consolidation Loan?

Most federal student loans and PLUS Loans (including FFEL program loans) can be consolidated. All the federal loans discussed are
eligible for consolidation. The Direct Loan Servicing Center can give you
a complete listing of eligible loans. The toll-free telephone number of the
Servicing Center's Consolidation Department is 1-800-848-0982.

FFEL CONSOLIDATION LOANS

An FFEL Consolidation Loan is designed to help student and parent
borrowers consolidate several types of federal student loans with various
repayment schedules into one loan. With an FFEL Consolidation Loan,
you'll make only one payment a month. FFEL Consolidation Loans are
available from participating lenders, such as banks, credit unions, and
savings and loan associations.

CAMPUS-BASED PROGRAMS

The three programs discussed in this section are called campus-based
programs because they're administered directly by the financial aid office
at each participating school. Not all schools participate in all three
programs. The Federal Supplemental Educational Opportunity Grant
(FSEOG) Program awards grants, the Federal Work-Study (FWS) Program offers jobs, and the Federal Perkins Loan Program offers loans.
Even though each program is different, they have these characteristics in
common:
    1. How much aid you receive depends on your financial need, on the
amount of other aid you'll receive, and the availability of funds at your
school. Unlike the Federal Pell Grant Program, which provides funds to
every eligible student, each school participating in any of the campus-
based programs receives a certain amount of funds for each campus-based
program each year. When that money is gone, no more awards can be
made from that program for that year.
    2. Each school sets its own deadlines for students to apply for campus-
based funds. The deadlines will usually be earlier than the U.S. Department of Education's deadline for filing a federal student financial aid

application (in this case, June 30, 1997). Ask your FAA about the school's deadlines. You may miss out on aid from these programs if you don't apply early!

V. FEDERAL SUPPLEMENTAL EDUCATIONAL OPPORTUNITY GRANTS

What Is a Federal Supplemental Educational Opportunity Grant?

A Federal Supplemental Educational Opportunity Grant (FSEOG) is for undergraduates with exceptional financial need, that is, students with the lowest Expected Family Contributions (EFCs), and gives priority to students who receive Federal Pell Grants. An FSEOG doesn't have to be paid back.

How Much Can I Get?

You can get between $100 and $4,000 a year, depending on when you apply, your level of need, and the funding level of the school you're attending.

VI. FEDERAL WORK-STUDY

What Is Federal Work-Study?

The Federal Work-Study (FWS) Program provides jobs for undergraduate and graduate students with financial need, allowing them to earn money to help pay education expenses. The program encourages community service work and work related to your course of study.

How Much Can I Make?

Your FWS salary will be at least the current federal minimum wage, but it may be higher, depending on the type of work you do and the skills required. Your total FWS award depends on when you apply, your level of need, and the funding level of your school.

VII. FEDERAL PERKINS LOANS

What Is a Federal Perkins Loan?

A Federal Perkins Loan is a low-interest (5 percent) loan for both undergraduate and graduate students with exceptional financial need. Your school is your lender and the loan is made with government funds. You must repay this loan to your school.

How Much Can I Borrow?

Depending on when you apply, your level of need, and the funding level of your school, you can borrow up to:
— $3,000 for each year of undergraduate study. The total amount you can borrow as an undergraduate is $15,000.
— $5,000 for each year of graduate or professional study. The total amount you can borrow as a graduate/professional student is $30,000. (This includes any Federal Perkins Loans you borrowed as an undergraduate.)

QUESTIONS YOU SHOULD NOT BE AFRAID TO ASK— YOU HAVE THE RIGHT TO RECEIVE THE FOLLOWING INFORMATION FROM THE SCHOOL:

— The financial assistance that is available, including information on all federal, state, local, private, and institutional financial aid programs.
— The procedures and deadlines for submitting applications for each available financial aid program.
— How a school selects financial aid recipients.
— How the school determines your financial need.
— How the school determines each type and amount of assistance in your financial aid package.
— How and when you'll receive your aid.
— How the school determines whether you're making satisfactory academic progress, and what happens if you're not.
— If you're offered a Federal Work-Study job, what the job is, what hours you must work, what your duties will be, what the rate of pay will be, and how and when you'll be paid.
— The location, hours, and counseling procedures of the school's financial aid office.

GLOSSARY OF TERMS

IMPORTANT TERMS USED BY THE U.S. DEPARTMENT OF EDUCATION

Academic Year: The time period schools use to measure a quantity of study. For example, a school's academic year may consist of a fall and spring semester, during which a student must complete 24 semester hours. Or it could consist of four quarters of six semester hours. Academic years vary from school to school, and even from educational program to educational program at the same school.

Citizenship: You must be one of the following to receive federal aid—
> U.S. Citizen
> U.S. National (includes natives of American
> > Samoa or Swain's Island)
> U.S. permanent resident who has an I-151,
> > I-551, or I-551C (Alien Registration
> > Receipt Card)

If you're not in one of these categories, you must have an Arrival-Departure Record (I-94) from the U.S. Immigration and Naturalization Service (INS) showing one of the following designations in order to be eligible:
> "Refugee"
> "Asylum Granted"
> "Indefinite Parole" and/or "Humanitarian Parole"
> "Cuban/Haitian Entrant, Status Pending"
> "Conditional Entrant" (valid only if issued
> > before April 1, 1980)
> Other eligible noncitizen with a Temporary
> > Resident Card (I-688)

Or you can be eligible based on the Family Unity Status category with an approved I-797 (Voluntary Departure and Immigrant Petition).

If you have only a Notice of Approval to Apply for Permanent Residence (I-171 or I-464), you aren't eligible for federal student aid.

If you're in the U.S. on a F1 or F2 student visa only, or on a J1 or J2 exchange visitor visa only, you can't get federal student aid. Also, persons with G series visas (pertaining to international organizations) are not eligible for federal student aid.

Citizens and eligible noncitizens may also receive loans from the FFEL and Direct Loan Programs at participating foreign schools.

Citizens of the Federated States of Micronesia, the Republic of the Marshall Islands, and Palau are eligible only for Federal Pell Grants, Federal Supplemental Educational Opportunity Grants (FSEOG), or Federal Work-Study (FWS). These applicants should check with their financial aid administrators for more information.

Cost of Attendance (COA): The total amount it will cost a student to go to school—usually expressed as a yearly figure. It is determined using rules established by the U.S. Congress. The COA includes tuition and fees; on-campus room and board (or a housing and food allowance for off-campus students); and allowances for books, supplies, transportation, loan fees (if applicable), dependent care, costs related to disability, and miscellaneous expenses. Also included are reasonable costs for eligible study abroad programs. An allowance (determined by the school) is included for reasonable costs connected with a student's employment as part of a cooperative education program. For students attending less than half time, the COA includes only tuition and fees and an allowance for books, supplies, transportation, and dependent-care expenses. Talk to the FAA at the school you're planning to attended if you have any unusual expenses that might affect your cost of attendance.

Default: Failure to repay a loan according to the terms agreed to when you signed a promissory note. Default also may result from failure to submit requests for deferment or cancellation on time. If you default, your school, the lender or agency that holds your loan, the state, and the federal government can take action to recover the money, including notifying national credit bureaus of your default. This notice may affect your credit rating for a long time, and you may find it very difficult to borrow from a bank to buy a car or a house. Furthermore, the lender or agency holding your loan may ask your employer to deduct payments from your paycheck. Also, you may be liable for expenses incurred in collecting the loan. If you decide to return to school, you're not entitled to receive any more federal student aid or any deferments. The U.S. Department of Education may ask the U.S. Internal Revenue Service to withhold your income tax refund, and the amount of your refund will be applied to what you owe.

Eligible Program: A course of study that leads to a degree or certificate and meets the U.S. Department of Education's requirements for an eligible program. To get federal financial aid, you must be enrolled in an eligible program, with two exceptions:

1. If a school has told you that you must take certain coursework to qualify for admission into one of its eligible programs, you can get a Direct Loan or an FFEL Loan (or your parents can get a PLUS Loan) for up to 12 consecutive months while you're completing that coursework. You must be enrolled at least half time, and you must meet the usual student aid eligibility requirements.

2. If you're enrolled at least half time in a program to obtain a professional credential or certification required by a state for employment as an elementary or secondary school teacher, you can get a Federal Perkins Loan, Federal Work-Study, an FFEL Stafford Loan, a Direct Loan (or your parents can get a PLUS Loan) while you're enrolled in that program.

Financial Aid Package: The total amount of financial aid (federal and nonfederal) a student receives.

General Education Development Certificate (GED): A certificate students receive if they've passed a specific, approved high school equivalency test. Students who don't have a high school diploma but who have a GED may still qualify for federal student aid. A school that admits students without a high school diploma must make a GED program in the vicinity of the school available to these students and must inform them about the program.

Guaranty Agency: The organization that administers the FFEL Program for your state. The federal government sets loan limits and interest rates, but each state is free to set its own additional limitations, within federal guidelines. This agency is the best source of information on FFEL Program Loans in your state. To find out the name, address, and telephone number of the agency serving your state, as well as information about borrowing, call the Federal Student Aid Information Center at 1-800-4-FED-AID (1-800-433-3243).

Half Time: At schools measuring progress by credit hours and semesters, trimesters, or quarters, half-time enrollment is at least 6 semester hours or quarter hours per term. At schools measuring progress by credit hours but not using semesters, trimesters, or quarters, half-time enrollment is at least 12 semester hours or 18 quarter hours per year. At schools measuring progress by clock hours, half-time enrollment is at least 12 hours per week. Note that schools may choose to set higher minimums than these.

You must be attending school at least half time to be eligible to receive Direct or FFEL Program Loans. Half-time enrollment is not a requirement to receive aid from the Federal Pell Grant, Federal Supplemental Educational Opportunity Grant (FSEOG), Federal Work-Study (FWS), and Federal Perkins Loan programs.

Promissory Note: The binding legal document you sign when you get a student loan. It lists the conditions under which you're borrowing and the terms under which you agree to pay back the loan. It will include information about your interest rate and about deferment and cancellation provisions. It's very important to read and save this document because you'll need to refer to it later when you begin repaying your loan.

Regular Student: One who is enrolled in an institution to obtain a degree or certificate. Generally, to receive aid from the programs discussed in this booklet, you must be a regular student. (For some programs, there are exceptions to this requirement. See the definition of eligible program.)

Satisfactory Academic Progress: To be eligible to receive federal student aid, you must maintain satisfactory academic progress toward a degree or certificate. You must meet your school's written standard of satisfactory progress. Check with your school to find out its standard.

If you received federal student aid for the first time on or after July 1, 1987, and you're enrolled in a program that's longer than two years, the following definition of satisfactory progress also applies to you: You must have a C average by the end of your second academic year of study or have an academic standing consistent with your institution's graduation requirements. You must continue to maintain satisfactory academic progress for the rest of your course of study.

Selective Service Registration: If required by law, you must register, or arrange to register, with the Selective Service to receive federal student aid. The requirement to register applies to males who were born on or after January 1, 1960, are at least 18 years old, are citizens or eligible non-citizens, and are not currently on active duty in the armed forces. (Citizens of the Federated States of Micronesia, the Marshall Islands, or Palau are exempt from registering.)

SOURCES OF INFORMATION

BOOKS

John B. Bear and Mariah P. Bear. *Bear's Guide to Finding Money for College*. Ten Speed Press, Berkeley, CA, 1993 ($7.95), 150 pages.

Laurie Blum. *Free Money for College from the Government*. Henry Holt, New York, 1st edition, 1993 ($14.95), 201 pages.

Laurie Blum. *Free Money for Private Schools*. Simon & Schuster, New York, 1992 ($12.00), 196 pages.

Daniel J. Cassidy and Michael J. Alves. *The Scholarship Book: The Complete Guide to Private-Sector Scholarships, Grants, and Loans for Undergraduates*. Prentice Hall, Englewood Cliffs, NJ, 4th edition, 1993 ($19.95), 400 pages.

Chronicle Financial Aid Guide 1993-94. Chronical Guidance Publications, Inc., Aurora, NY, 1993 ($19.97 plus $2 postage and handling).

Andy Clark and Amy Clark. *Athletic Scholarships: Thousands of Grants and Over $400 Million for College-Bound Athletes*. Facts on File, New York, 3rd edition, 1994 ($14.95), 320 pages.

Financial Aid for Minority Students in Health Fields. Garrett Park Press, Garrett Park, MD, 1993 ($4.95).

Mark Kantrowitz and Joann P. DiGennaro. *Prentice Hall Guide to Scholarships and Fellowships for Math and Science Students*. Prentice Hall, Englewood Cliffs, NJ, 1993 ($19.95), 325 pages.

Oreon Keeslar and Judy Keeslar Santamari. *Financial Aids for Higher Education*. Brown & Benchmark, Madison, WI, 16th edition, 1995 ($35.00), 688 pages.

Debra M. Kirby and Christa Brelin. *Fund Your Way Through College: Uncovering 1,700 Great Opportunities in Undergraduate Financial Aid*. Visible Ink Press, Detroit, MI, 1994 ($19.95), 731 pages.

Cynthia Ruiz McKee and Phillip C. McKee, Jr. *Ca$h for College: The Ultimate Guide to College Scholarships*. Hearst Books, New York, 1st edition, 1993 ($16.95), 510 pages.

Marianne Ragins. *Winning Scholarships for College: An Insider's Guide*. Henry Holt and Co., New York, NY, 1994 ($10.95).

NEWSLETTERS

The Black Student Advisor. Beckham House Publishers, Inc., P.O. Box 8008, Silver Spring, MD 20907. Bimonthly report on programs and services for black students, including updated financial aid opportunities. $36 yearly for families, $75 for institutions.

INTERNET

Black Excel: The College Help Network includes a guide to historically black colleges and has a list of more than 350 grants and scholarships for African-American students. e-mail to: ijblack@cnct.com.

College Prep Page collects resources for planning as well as provides information about financial aid, admissions, and career planning: http://www.tpoint.net/~jewels/college.html.

College SAT and Financial Aid Planning Service supplies FAF forms, Plus Loans applications, and SAT courses: http://www.tiac.net/users/online/college.

Financial Aid Information Page, Mark Kantrowitz (e-mail: mkant@cs.cmu.edu). Provides links to sources of financial aid: http://www.cs.cmu.edu/~finaid/finaid.html.

fastWEB (Financial Aid Search Through the WEB) offers a free searchable database of more than 180,000 private aid sources: http://www.studentservices.com/fastweb.

Money for College gives assistance in finding money for higher education: http://emporium.turnpike.net/D/dcservice/wg/lenn4.htm.

GUIDE TO SCHOLARSHIPS

[001] ACHE, ALBERT W. DENT SCHOLARSHIP
ELIGIBILITY: Awarded to a minority student for full-time study in a graduate program of healthcare management. Student must be a U.S. citizen. Deadline March 31.
AMOUNT: $3,000
CONTACT: Foundation of American College Healthcare Executives, Attn: Albert W. Dent Scholarship, 1 North Franklin Street, Suite 1700, Chicago, IL 60606-3461, (312) 943-0544.

[002] ADHA INSTITUTE
ELIGIBILITY: The minority scholarship is available to students enrolled in certificate/associate or bachelor's degree dental hygiene programs. Must have a 3.0 GPA and show financial need. Deadline May 1.
AMOUNT: $1,500
CONTACT: ADHA Institute for Oral Health, 444 N. Michigan Avenue, Suite 3400, Chicago, IL 60611, (312) 440-8900.

[003] AFNA NEW ACCESS ROUTES TO PROFESSIONAL CAREERS
ELIGIBILITY: Primarily for black high school students who have completed the 10th grade and who are residents of Philadelphia. Program is aimed at placing students at medical schools or laboratories to get research experience and earn money for college.
AMOUNT: Varies
CONTACT: American Foundation for Negro Affairs, 1700 Market Street, Philadelphia, PA 19103, (215) 563-1248.

[004] AFRICAN METHODIST EPISCOPAL CHURCH
ELIGIBILITY: Scholarships are available through local congregations. The AME church has over 8,000 congregations worldwide.
AMOUNT: Varies
CONTACT: African Methodist Episcopal Church, 2311 N St., NW, Washington, DC 20037, (202) 337-3930.

[005] AFRICAN METHODIST EPISCOPAL ZION CHURCH

ELIGIBILITY: This organization's 1.5 million members, encompassing 2,500 churches, provides scholarships for its college-bound members.
AMOUNT: Varies
CONTACT: African Methodist Episcopal Zion Church, 1200 Windermere Drive, Pittsburgh, PA 15218, (412) 242-5842.

[006] AICPA SCHOLARSHIPS FOR MINORITY UNDERGRADUATE ACCOUNTING MAJORS

ELIGIBILITY: Applicants must be minority students who are undergraduate accounting majors, U.S. citizens or permanent residents, and in financial need.
AMOUNT: Up to $1,500
CONTACT: Sharon Donahue, Manager, Minority Recruitment, American Institute of Certified Public Accountants, 1211 Avenue of the Americas, New York, NY 10036, (212) 575-7641.

[007] AICPA MINORITY DOCTORAL FELLOWSHIPS

ELIGIBILITY: Full-time minority students in doctoral accounting programs. Fellowships contingent upon acceptance of the candidate into a doctoral program in a recognized school of business. Must have a master's degree or completed a minimum of three years, full-time experience in accounting. Deadline April 1.
AMOUNT: $12,000 renewable
CONTACT: Minority Doctoral Fellowships, American Institute of Certified Public Accountants, 1211 Avenue of the Americas, New York, NY 10036-8775, (212) 596-6200.

[008] AICPA MINORITY SCHOLARSHIPS

ELIGIBILITY: Full-time minority students at a four-year accredited institution. Must have a minimum of 30 credit hours that include six hours in accounting with a minimum 3.0 GPA. Deadline July 1.
AMOUNT: up to $5,000
CONTACT: Minority Doctoral Fellowships, American Institute of

Certified Public Accountants, 1211 Avenue of the Americas, New York, NY 10036-8775, (212) 596-6200.

---

[009] UNIVERSITY OF AKRON

ELIGIBILITY: The Janet B. Purnell and W. Howard Fort Scholarship is awarded to entering black students with a 3.0 GPA.
AMOUNT: $1,500
CONTACT: Director of Minority Affairs, Office of Minority Affairs, University of Akron, 302 E. Buchtel Avenue, Akron, OH 44325, (216) 375-7658.

---

[010] UNIVERSITY OF ALABAMA/HUNTSVILLE SCHOLARSHIP

ELIGIBILITY: Must be a U.S. citizen, majoring in engineering. Renewable with a 3.0 GPA. Financial need required. Deadline December 3.
AMOUNT: $1,965
CONTACT: Admissions Office, University of Alabama, 124 University Center, Huntsville, AL 35899, (204) 894-6070.

---

[011] ALFRED P. SLOAN FOUNDATION

ELIGIBILITY: Minority students who have completed their junior year in college and who are interested in government careers. Students must attend accredited summer institute. Deadline varies.
AMOUNT: $6,000
CONTACT: APAM Program, Alfred P. Sloan Foundation, 630 Fifth Avenue, Suite 2550, New York, NY 10111, (212) 582-0450.

---

[012] ALLIED DAILY NEWSPAPER SCHOLARSHIP PROGRAM

ELIGIBILITY: Students interested in majoring in journalism should contact the Allied Daily Newspaper for more information on their scholarship programs: Cascade Bldg., Tribune Business Park, 19th & Trafton; P.O. Box 11128; Tacoma, WA 98411-0128.
AMOUNT: Varies

CONTACT: Scholarship Committee, Allied Daily Newspaper, P.O. Box 11128, Tacoma, WA 98411-0128, (206) 272-3611.

[013] ALLIED DAILY NEWSPAPER FOUNDATION JOURNALISM SCHOLARSHIP FOR MINORITY STUDENTS
ELIGIBILITY: Applicants must be majoring in journalism and residing in or attending a 4-year college or university in Alaska, Idaho, Montana, Oregon, or Washington. Financial need required.
AMOUNT: $1,100
CONTACT: Allied Daily Newspaper Foundation, P.O. Box 11410, Tacoma, WA 98411, (206) 272-3611.

[014] ALPHA KAPPA ALPHA SORORITY
ELIGIBILITY: Many of the 700 local chapters offer scholarships to qualified high school and college students. Awards are almost exclusively for black women.
AMOUNT: Varies
CONTACT: Alpha Kappa Alpha Sorority, Inc., 5211 So. Greenwood Avenue, Chicago, IL 60615, (312) 684-1282.

[015] ALPHA PHI ALPHA FRATERNITY
ELIGIBILITY: The fraternity provides scholarships to high school students involved in various educational and community projects.
AMOUNT: Varies
CONTACT: Alpha Phi Alpha Fraternity, Inc., 4432 So. Martin Luther King Drive, Chicago, IL 60653, (312) 373-1819.

[016] ALPHA PHI ALPHA FRATERNITY
ELIGIBILITY: Paul Robeson Scholarship Preference will be given to students who have exhibited the potential and desire to further their education and need financial assistance. Male minority students are encouraged to apply. Deadline March 21.
AMOUNT: Varies

CONTACT: Scholarship Coordinator, Alpha Phi Alpha Fraternity, Iota Upsilon Lambda Chapter, P.O. Box 2233, Silver Spring, MD 20902, (301) 727-5947.

[017] ALVERNO COLLEGE AETNA LIFE & CASUALTY FOUNDATION SCHOLARSHIP GRANT

ELIGIBILITY: Designed to help qualified minorities who, without such financial assistance, would possibly be unable to further their education.
AMOUNT: Varies
CONTACT: Alverno College, Office of Student Financial Planning and Resources, 3401 South 39 Street, Milwaukee, WI 53215, (414) 382-6000.

[018] ALVERNO COLLEGE BRUNSWICK PUBLIC CHARITABLE FOUNDATION

ELIGIBILITY: Scholarships for minority Weekend College students.
AMOUNT: Varies
CONTACT: Alverno College, Office of Student Financial Planning and Resources, 3401 South 39 Street, Milwaukee, WI 53215, (414) 382-6000.

[019] ALVERNO COLLEGE CRAY RESEARCH FOUNDATION

ELIGIBILITY: Scholarship money for minority students majoring in computer science or related disciplines.
AMOUNT: Varies
CONTACT: Alverno College, Office of Student Financial Planning and Resources, 3401 South 39 Street, Milwaukee, WI 53215, (414) 382-6000.

[020] ALVERNO COLLEGE GARDNER SCHOLARSHIP
ELIGIBILITY: Full-tuition scholarship for a Hispanic woman.
AMOUNT: Varies
CONTACT: Alverno College, Office of Student Financial Planning and Resources, 3401 South 39 Street, Milwaukee, WI 53215, (414) 382-6000.

**[021] ALVERNO COLLEGE KRAFT FOUNDATION
        SCHOLARSHIP**
ELIGIBILITY: Kraft Foundation Scholarship Award is for minority students who meet scholarship standards. New incoming students must participate in a scholarship opportunity day in order to be considered for scholarships.
AMOUNT: $1,800
CONTACT: Director of Financial Aid, Alverno College, Office of Financial Aid, 3401 South 39 Street, Milwaukee, WI 53215, (414) 382-6046.

[022] ALVERNO COLLEGE MARK SCHOLARSHIP
ELIGIBILITY: Minority students who meet Alverno's scholarship standards.
AMOUNT: Varies
CONTACT: Alverno College, Office of Student Financial Planning and Resources, 3401 South 39 Street, Milwaukee, WI 53215, (414) 382-6000.

**[023] ALVERNO COLLEGE SCHUMANN
        SCHOLARSHIP**
ELIGIBILITY: Minority students who meet Alverno's scholarship standards.
AMOUNT: Varies
CONTACT: Alverno College, Office of Student Financial Planning and Resources, 3401 South 39 Street, Milwaukee, WI 53215, (414) 382-6000.

[024] ALVERNO COLLEGE WISCONSIN BELL SCHOLARSHIP

ELIGIBILITY: Minority student specializing in technological areas.
AMOUNT: Varies
CONTACT: Alverno College, Office of Student Financial Planning and Resources, 3401 South 39 Street, Milwaukee, WI 53215, (414) 382-6000.

[025] AMERICAN DENTAL HYGIENISTS' ASSOCIATION

ELIGIBILITY: Minority students enrolled in a dental hygiene program. Applicants must have completed a minimum of one year in dental hygiene curriculum and have a 3.0 GPA. Minimum financial need of $1500. Deadline June 1.
AMOUNT: Varies
CONTACT: Minority Scholarships, American Dental Hygienists' Association, Institute for Oral Health, 444 N. Michigan Avenue, Suite 3400, Chicago, IL 60611, (312) 440-8900.

[026] AMERICAN FUND FOR DENTAL HEALTH

ELIGIBILITY: Minority Dental Student Scholarship. Minority first-year dental students attending a dental school in the U.S. accredited by the Commission on Dental Accreditation. Must demonstrate financial need, personal commitment to dentistry, school, and community services, activities, and awards. Deadline May 1.
AMOUNT: $1,000 - $2,000
CONTACT: Program Department, American Fund for Dental Health, 211 E. Chicago Avenue, Suite 820, Chicago, IL 60611, (312) 787-6270.

[027] AMERICAN FUND FOR DENTAL HEALTH DENTAL SCHOLARSHIPS FOR MINORITY STUDENTS

ELIGIBILITY: Applicants must have been accepted by a dental school in the U.S. which is accredited by the Commission on Dental Accreditation. Consideration will be given on academic performance, demonstrated

financial need, personal commitment to dentistry, school and community service, activities and awards, and character references. Applications are available from the Student Affairs or Financial Aid office of the dental school to be attended. Applicants must submit the following: official application form, official transcripts of all college records, letter of acceptance from an accredited dental school, three letters of reference including one from an official of the dental school attesting to the applicant's character, personality, and academic ability, a financial needs statement, and the scores from the dental aptitude test. Deadline April 15.
AMOUNT: Varies
CONTACT: American Fund for Dental Health, 211 E. Chicago Avenue, Suite 820, Chicago, IL 60611, (312) 787-6270.

---

[028] AMERICAN GEOLOGICAL INSTITUTE
ELIGIBILITY: Geoscience majors currently enrolled in accredited institutions as either undergraduate or graduate students are eligible to apply. Awards are based on academic excellence, need, and probable future success in the broad family of geoscience professions. Applicant must be a U.S. citizen.
AMOUNT: $250 to $1,500
CONTACT: University of New Orleans, Dept. of Geology/ Geophysiology, New Orleans, LA 70148.

---

[029] AMERICAN GEOLOGICAL INSTITUTE, MINORITY PARTICIPATION
ELIGIBILITY: Judged on academic achievement, financial need, and potential for success. Must be a U.S. citizen and majoring in one of the following; geology, meteorology, geochemistry, planetary geology, geophysics, oceanography, hydrology or earth sciences. Deadline February 1.
AMOUNT: Varies
CONTACT: Director of Education, American Geological Institute, 4220 King Street, Alexandria, VA 22302, (703) 379-2480.

---

[030] AMERICAN HOME ECONOMICS ASSOCIATION
ELIGIBILITY: The Freda DeKnight Fellowship is available to a black American graduate student. Preference is given to qualified applicants who plan to study in home economics communications or work in cooperative extension. A $10.00 application fee must accompany each request for fellowship materials.
AMOUNT: $1,500
CONTACT: American Home Economics Association, 2010 Massachusetts Avenue, NW, Washington, DC 20036-1028, (202) 862-8300.

[031] AMERICAN HOME ECONOMICS ASSOCIATION
ELIGIBILITY: The Flemmie P. Kittrell Fellowship is offered for graduate study for members of minority groups in the U.S. and developing countries. A $10.00 application fee must accompany each request for fellowship materials. Deadline January 15. Must be majoring in home economics.
AMOUNT: $3,000
CONTACT: American Home Economics Association, 2010 Massachusetts Avenue, NW, Washington, DC 20036-1028, (202) 862-8300.

[032] AMERICAN INSTITUTE OF ARCHITECTS
ELIGIBILITY: Minority/Disadvantaged Scholarship Program awards scholarships renewable for three years. Students should be nominated by an architect or a counselor.
AMOUNT: $400 to $3,000
CONTACT: Mary Felber, American Institute of Architects, 1735 New York Avenue, NW, Washington, DC 20006, (202) 626-7300.

[033] AMERICAN INSTITUTE OF ARCHITECTS
ELIGIBILITY: Minority Program. Must be nominated and be a U.S. citizen. Must not have completed first year of a 4 year program. Deadline January 15.
AMOUNT: Varies
CONTACT: Education Program Director, American Institute of Architects, 1735 New York Avenue, NW, Washington, DC 20006, (202) 626-7353.

[034] AMERICAN LIBRARY ASSOCIATION

ELIGIBILITY: Louise Giles Minority Scholarship. Applicant must not have completed more than 12 semester hours and be enrolled in a library school offering an American Library Association accredited program. Applicants must be U.S. or Canadian citizens.
AMOUNT: $3,000
CONTACT: American Library Association, 50 E. Huron Street, Chicago, IL 60611, (312) 944-6780.

[035] AMERICAN LIBRARY ASSOCIATION

ELIGIBILITY: LITA/OCLC Minority Scholarship in Library and Information Technology. Minorities interested in pursuing a master's degree in an ALA-accredited program.
AMOUNT: $2,500
CONTACT: American Library Association, 50 E. Huron Street, Chicago, IL 60611, (312) 944-6780.

[036] AMERICAN NURSES' ASSOCIATION BACCALAUREATE COMPLETION SCHOLARSHIP PROGRAM

ELIGIBILITY: This program is designed for, but not limited to, minority R.N.'s interested in pursuing full-time study towards a Baccalaureate degree in nursing. Recipients must be enrolled in an accredited Baccalaureate Nursing Program. Deadline January
AMOUNT: $2,000
CONTACT: American Nurses' Association Minority Fellowship Programs, 600 Maryland Avenue, SW, Suite 100W, Washington, DC 20024-2571, (202) 651-7246.

[037] AMERICAN NURSES' ASSOCIATION CLINICAL FELLOWSHIP PROGRAM FOR ETHNIC/RACIAL MINORITIES

ELIGIBILITY: Fellowship is for doctoral study in psychiatric nursing. Applicants must be U.S. citizens or permanent residents. Deadline January 15.

AMOUNT: $7,500
CONTACT: American Nurses' Association, Ethnic/Racial Minority Fellowship Program, 2420 Pershing Road, Kansas City, MO 64108, (816) 474-5720.

---

[038] AMERICAN PHYSICAL SOCIETY
ELIGIBILITY: APS Minorities Scholarship Program. Minority high school seniors or college freshman and sophomores majoring in physics. Applicants must complete application and personal statement as well as provide references, official transcripts, and standardized test scores. Deadline February 17.
AMOUNT: $2,000 renewable
CONTACT: The American Physical Society, One Physics Ellipse, College Park, MD 20740-3844, (301) 209-3200.

---

[039] AMERICAN PHYSICAL SOCIETY CORPORATE SPONSORED SCHOLARSHIPS FOR MINORITY UNDERGRADUATE STUDENTS IN PHYSICS
ELIGIBILITY: Awards sponsored by corporations and given to outstanding minority students who are or plan to major in physics.
AMOUNT: $2,000
CONTACT: The American Physical Society, One Physics Ellipse, College Park, MD 20740-3844, (301) 209-3200.

---

[040] AMERICAN PLANNING ASSOCIATION
ELIGIBILITY: Planning Fellowship Program. Must be enrolled in a recognized graduate program and nominated by school. Deadline May 15.
AMOUNT: $2,000 to $5,000
CONTACT: Director of Council Programs, American Planning Association, 1776 Massachusetts Avenue, NW, Washington, DC 20036, (202) 872-0611.

---

[041] AMERICAN POLITICAL SCIENCE ASSOCIATION
ELIGIBILITY: Black Graduate Fellowship Program. Applicants should be able to successfully pursue a doctoral degree in political science. Applicants with the greatest financial need will be given preference.
AMOUNT: $6,000
CONTACT: American Political Science Association, 1527 New Hampshire Avenue, NW, Washington, DC 20036, (202) 483-2512.

[042] AMERICAN PSYCHOLOGICAL ASSOCIATION
ELIGIBILITY: APA Minority Fellowship Program in Clinical Training. Applicants must be U.S. citizens or permanent residents, enrolled full-time in an accredited doctoral program committed to a career in psychology related to ethnic minority mental health. Selection is based on clinical and/or research potential, scholarship, writing ability, ethnic minority identification, knowledge of broad issues in psychology, and professional commitment. Students of clinical and counseling psychology and students working on a master's degree only are ineligible. Recipients are obligated to provide clinical services to underserved populations within 24 months after the completion of their training and for a period equal to the length of the award. This obligation may not be fulfilled in private clinical practice. Deadline January.
AMOUNT: Varies
CONTACT: American Psychological Association, Attn: Minority Fellowship Program, 750 First Street, NE, Washington, DC 20002-4242, (202) 336-5500.

[043] AMERICAN PSYCHOLOGY ASSOCIATION
ELIGIBILITY: Minority Fellowship Program. For a minority research-science student. Deadline January 15.
AMOUNT: Varies
CONTACT: APA Minority Fellowship Program, 1200 17th Street, NW, Washington, DC 20036, (913) 864-3881.

[044] AMERICAN SOCIETY FOR MICROBIOLOGY

ELIGIBILITY: Pre-doctoral Minority Fellowship is awarded to U.S. minority citizens who are formally admitted as fully qualified prospective candidates for a Ph.D. degree in microbiology in an accredited institution in the United States. Financial need required. Deadline May 1.
AMOUNT: $9,250
CONTACT: Public Affairs Director, American Society for Microbiology, 1325 Massachusetts Avenue, NW, Washington, DC 20005, (202) 833-9680.

[045] AMERICAN SOCIOLOGICAL ASSOCIATION

ELIGIBILITY: Minority Fellowship Program is for minority American citizens and permanent visa residents in a full-time sociology doctoral program. The purpose of the award is to contribute to the development of sociology by recruiting persons who will add differing orientations and creativity to the field. Deadline December 31.
AMOUNT: $10,008 plus tuition
CONTACT: Minority Fellowship Program, American Sociological Association, 1722 N Street, NW, Washington, DC 20036, (202) 833-3410, Fax: (202) 785-0146.

[046] AMERICAN SPEECH-LANGUAGE-HEARING
FOUNDATION

ELIGIBILITY: Kala Singh Memorial Priority is given to applicants who are foreign or minority students studying communication sciences in the continental U.S. The student must be accepted for graduate study in an ASLH Educational Standards Board accredited program, must be enrolled for full-time study, must be in need of financial aid, must be in good academic standing, must be recommended by a committee of two or more persons, and must not have received a prior scholarship from the American Speech-Language-Hearing Foundation. Deadline June 15.
AMOUNT: $2,000
CONTACT: Scholarship Committee, American Speech-Language-Hearing Foundation, 10801 Rockville Pike, Rockville, MD 20852, (301) 897-5700.

[047] AMERICAN SPEECH-LANGUAGE-HEARING FOUNDATION

ELIGIBILITY: Young Scholars Award. This student must be a college senior who has been accepted for full-time study in a graduate program in speech-language pathology or audiology for the forthcoming academic term. The student must also be a U.S. citizen and a racial/ethnic minority. The student must submit an original scholarly paper. Must be majoring in one of the following: speech pathology, speech/hearing, speech or speech therapy. Deadline May 1.
AMOUNT: $2,000
CONTACT: Scholarship Committee, American Speech-Language-Hearing Foundation, 10801 Rockville Pike, Rockville, MD 20852, (301) 897-5700.

[048] AMERICAN UNIVERSITY

ELIGIBILITY: The Hechinger Foundation Scholarship. First preference is given to a black undergraduate student from the District of Columbia who is majoring in business. Deadline March 1.
AMOUNT: Varies
CONTACT: American University, 4400 Massachusetts Avenue, NW, Washington, DC 20016, (202) 885-6100.

[049] AMERICAN UNIVERSITY

ELIGIBILITY: Special Opportunity Grants are awarded to American born graduate students for up to 24 semester hours of tuition remission per year and/or a stipend for a service commitment. Deadline March 1.
AMOUNT: Varies
CONTACT: Graduate Affairs Office, American University, 4400 Massachusetts Avenue, NW, Washington, DC 20016, (202) 885-6100.

[050] AMERICAN UNIVERSITY

ELIGIBILITY: The Frederick Douglass Scholarship is available to undergraduate students who have graduated from a District of Columbia high school and who demonstrate academic achievement and financial need. The scholarship ranges from partial to full tuition for recipients who

are enrolled on a full-time basis. The Frederick Douglass Scholarship program is open only to applicants who are U.S. citizens and persons who hold permanent resident status. The applicant must be admissible to an undergraduate degree program at the American University and must have significant financial need. Students seeking admission should have at least a 2.5 GPA on a 4.0 scale, rank in the top half of their graduating class, and have acceptable SAT or ACT scores. Deadline February 1.
AMOUNT: Varies
CONTACT: Financial Aid Director, American University, 4400 Massachusetts Avenue, NW, Washington, DC 20016, (202) 885-6100.

[051] ANTIOCH COLLEGE
ELIGIBILITY: Alfred Hampton Memorial Scholarships. Minorities with strong academic records and demonstrated qualities of creativity. Must submit an essay about a challenging experience. Deadline February 1.
AMOUNT: Up to $5,000
CONTACT: Office of Admissions, Antioch College, Yellow Springs, OH 45387, (513) 757-6400.

[052] ANTIOCH COLLEGE
ELIGIBILITY: Antioch Minority Science Scholarships. Applicants must be a science major with a strong academic record and an interest in exploring the relationship between science and society. Deadline January 31.
AMOUNT: Full tuition
CONTACT: Office of Admissions, Antioch College, Yellow Springs, OH 45387, (800) 543-9436 outside Ohio, (513) 767-7047 call collect inside Ohio.

[053] ANTIOCH COLLEGE
ELIGIBILITY: Atlanta Scholarships. Applicants must be an Atlanta area resident with a strong academic record. Deadline January 31.
AMOUNT: Full tuition
CONTACT: Office of Admissions, Antioch College, Yellow Springs,

OH 45387, (800) 543-9436 outside Ohio, (513) 767-7047 call collect inside Ohio.

---

[054] ANTIOCH COLLEGE

ELIGIBILITY: Horace Mann Scholarships. Applicants must have a strong record as an activist on behalf of humanitarian values (e.g. peace, civil rights, environment) with a strong academic record. Deadline January 31.
AMOUNT: Full tuition
CONTACT: Office of Admissions, Antioch College, Yellow Springs, OH 45387, (800) 543-9436 outside Ohio, (513) 767-7047 call collect inside Ohio.

---

[055] ANTIOCH COLLEGE

ELIGIBILITY: Upward Bound Scholarships. Applicants must have been a participant in Upward Bound or similar program, and have a strong academic background. A separate admissions and scholarship application must be completed. The student must also go through a personal interview. Deadline January 15.
AMOUNT: Full tuition
CONTACT: Office of Admissions, Antioch College, Yellow Springs, OH 45387, (800) 543-9436 outside Ohio, (513) 767-7047 call collect inside Ohio.

---

[056] APPALACHIAN STATE UNIVERSITY

ELIGIBILITY: The Minority Presence Grant is available to black North Carolina residents who enroll in a degree program on at least a half-time basis. Applicants must be entering freshman who demonstrate exceptional financial need. Students may apply by completing the university's application for student financial aid and the financial aid form. Deadline March 15.
AMOUNT: Varies
CONTACT: Financial Aid Director, Appalachian State University, Boone, NC 28608, (704) 262-2190.

---

[057] ARCF

ELIGIBILITY: The Jimmy Young Scholarships—Respiratory Care. Applicants must be U.S. citizens or have visas, be of a minority origin, be enrolled in an American Medical Association-approved respiratory care program, demonstrate financial need, submit at least 2 letters of recommendation attesting to worthiness and potential in the field (one from program director or senior faculty member, and one from medical director), and submit an original referenced paper on some facet of respiratory care.

AMOUNT: $1000

CONTACT: American Respiratory Care Foundation, 11030 Ables Lane, Dallas, TX 75229, (214) 243-2272.

[058] ARISTO CLUB OF BOSTON

ELIGIBILITY: Competitive Scholarship. Applicants must be a black senior high school student in a Massachusetts high school who is entering a college or university in the fall and has at least a B average. The application must be in the form of a letter, signed by the applicant, and containing the following information: 1) Name, address, and telephone number; 2) Date of birth; 3) Parent's names or person in loco-parentis; 4) School attending and course pursuing; 5) School, church, and community activities; and 6) Reasons for desiring a college education. A transcript of high school record must be filed with the application together with certified rank from the principal or headmaster. The applicant must submit at least three letters of recommendation from three reliable persons. Applicants are advised to follow through personally on these references as no application will be considered complete without them. Consideration for the award will be limited to the first twenty eligible applications received. Applicants will be notified of the time and place for an interview. Among the topics for discussion during the interview will be current events, individual background for chosen course, and personal community participation. Deadline April 20.

AMOUNT: Varies

CONTACT: Aristo Club of Boston, 193 Fayerweather Street, Cambridge, MA 02138.

[059] UNIVERSITY OF ARKANSAS

ELIGIBILITY: The Minority Incentive Tuition Grant is awarded to black students. Applicants must be a U.S. citizen. Deadline is June 1.
AMOUNT: $1,000
CONTACT: Graduate School Dean, University of Arkansas, Office of Financial Aid, 2801 S. University, Little Rock, AR 72204, (501) 569-3206.

[060] ARMCO MINORITIES ENGINEERING SCHOLARSHIPS

ELIGIBILITY: Black students who are planning to major in engineering, rank in the top third of their class, and are residents of a community where a participating Armco facility is located.
AMOUNT: $2,000
CONTACT: Armco Insurance Group, 703 Curtis Street, Middletown, OH 45043, (513) 425-5293.

[061] ARMCO MINORITIES IN INSURANCE AND RISK MANAGEMENT SCHOLARSHIP

ELIGIBILITY: Black seniors who rank in the top half of their class, and plan to major in business. Applicants must reside in a community where a participating Armco facility is located.
AMOUNT: $2,000
CONTACT: Armco Insurance Group, 703 Curtis Street, Middletown, OH 45043, (513) 425-5293.

[062] ARMSTRONG WORLD INDUSTRIES

ELIGIBILITY: Multicultural Education Scholarships. Minorities who are college juniors majoring in business, engineering, information systems, chemistry, or accounting with a cumulative 3.0 GPA and participation in school activities. Applicants must attend a college where Armstrong recruits (check school's financial aid office for more information). Deadline is the first quarter of each calendar year.
AMOUNT: Varies
CONTACT: Multicultural Education Scholarships, Armstrong World Industries, P.O. Box 3001, Lancaster, PA 17604.

[063] ARMY ROTC QUALITY ENRICHMENT PROGRAM

ELIGIBILITY: Must be a black U.S. citizen and be physically fit and have good grades. Will be commissioned as an officer after graduation. Deadline December 1.
AMOUNT: $200 a year
CONTACT: Army ROTC QEP, 11499 Chester, Suite 403, Cincinnati, OH 45246, (513) 772-6135.

[064] ARTURO SCHOMBURG SCHOLARSHIP

ELIGIBILITY: Awarded to students of color who show promise of strong academic performance and who exhibit potential for leadership at Hampshire College and in their own communities. Applicants must demonstrate financial need and be in upper twenty-percent of class. Renewable for four years.
AMOUNT: Ten awards of $3,000 to $7,500
CONTACT: Hampshire College, Attn: Financial Aid Director, Amherst, MA 01002, (413) 582-5484.

[065] ASSOCIATION OF BLACK JOURNALISTS SCHOLARSHIP PROGRAM

ELIGIBILITY: Applicants must have participated in the annual St. Louis Minority Journalism Workshop, be black college students majoring in journalism, and live in the St. Louis area.
AMOUNT: $1,000
CONTACT: National Association of Black Journalists, Greater St. Louis Area Chapter, 2953 Dr. Martin Luther King Drive, St. Louis, MO, 63106, (314) 535-5185.

[066] AT&T BELL LABORATORIES

ELIGIBILITY: Cooperative Research Fellowship Program. Minority graduate students who are working toward Ph.D. programs in engineering, chemistry, physics, statistics, and other areas. Deadline January 15.
AMOUNT: Full tuition, plus renewable $13,200 stipend, summer internships included

CONTACT: ESP Manager, AT&T Bell Laboratories, 600 Mountain Avenue, RM3D-303, P.O. Box 636, Murray Hill, NJ 07974-0636, (908) 582-6461.

---

[067] AT&T BELL LABORATORIES ENGINEERING SCHOLARSHIPS

ELIGIBILITY: Applicants must be minority students with a 3.0 GPA majoring in electrical or mechanical engineering or computer science. Deadline January 15.
AMOUNT: Tuition and fees
CONTACT: ESP Manager, AT&T Bell Laboratories, 600 Mountain Avenue, RM3D-303, P.O. Box 636, Munray Hill, NJ 07974-0636, (908) 582-6461.

---

[068] AURORA UNIVERSITY PRESIDENTIAL MINORITY ACHIEVEMENT SCHOLARSHIP

ELIGIBILITY: Graduating minority high school seniors entering Aurora University as full-time students with strong SAT and ACT scores.
AMOUNT: Tuition, room and board
CONTACT: Aurora University, Attn: Office of University Admissions, 347 S. Gladstone Avenue, Aurora, IL 60506-4892, (708) 896-1975.

---

[069] BALL STATE UNIVERSITY

ELIGIBILITY: Academic Recognition Award. Awarded to out-of-state minority high school seniors who have a cumulative 3.0 GPA, rank in the top 50 percent of their class, and have taken a college preparatory curriculum.
AMOUNT: $4,380
CONTACT: Ball State University, Attn: Office of Scholarships and Financial Aid, Lucina Hall, Room 245, Muncie, IN 47306, (317) 285-5600.

---

[070] BALL STATE UNIVERSITY
ELIGIBILITY: Library Science Scholarship. These library training fellowship grants are provided by the U.S. Dept. of Education.
AMOUNT: $8,000
CONTACT: Library Science Department, Ball State University, 2000 University Avenue, Muncie, IN 47306, (317) 285-5900.

[071] BALL STATE UNIVERSITY
ELIGIBILITY: Holmes/McFadden Memorial awards a minority student majoring in journalism. Deadline February 15.
AMOUNT: $1,000
CONTACT: Ball State University, Attn: Journalism Department, 2000 University Avenue, Muncie, IN 47306, (317) 285-8200.

[072] BALTIMORE SUN SCHOLARSHIP FOR MINORITY JOURNALISTS
ELIGIBILITY: Applicants must be enrolled in a four-year institution and have a minimum 3.5 GPA. Preference to Maryland students. Deadline December 30.
AMOUNT: $7,500
CONTACT: Human Resources Administration, The Baltimore Sun, 501 N. Calvert Street, P.O. Box 1377, Baltimore, MD 21278-0001, (301) 332-6268.

[073] BAPTIST GENERAL CONVENTION OF TEXAS
ELIGIBILITY: Texas Black Baptist Scholarship Program. Applicant must be a black American, a member of a Baptist church, a graduate of a Texas school, and recommended by a pastor and teacher. In addition, the applicant must have maintained a B average in high school, given evidence of being a "genuine Christian," possess a "vital interest in the advancement of the Kingdom of God," and attend a Texas Baptist educational institution agreed upon by the scholarship committee.
AMOUNT: up to $800
CONTACT: Baptist General Convention of Texas, 511 North Akard, Suite 1013, Dallas, TX, 75201-3355, (214) 741-1991.

[074] BARBER-SCOTIA COLLEGE
ELIGIBILITY: The United Negro College Fund is awarded to entering black students. Must have a strong academic background. Apply early.
AMOUNT: $100 to $2,000
CONTACT: Financial Aid Office, Barber-Scotia College, 145 Cabarrus Avenue, Concord, NC 28025, (704) 786-5171.

[075] BENTLEY COLLEGE
ELIGIBILITY: Freshman Minority Awards are limited to eight semesters. Must be a U.S. citizen and show financial need.
AMOUNT: Full tuition
CONTACT: Scholarship Coordinator, Bentley College, Admissions Office, Waltham, MA 02254, (617) 891-2244.

[076] BENTLEY COLLEGE
ELIGIBILITY: Upperclass Minority Grant. Student must be a U.S. citizen, show need and have family income below $30,000. Minimum GPA of 2.0.
AMOUNT: Varies
CONTACT: Scholarship Coordinator, Bentley College, Financial Aid Office, Waltham, MA 02254 , (617) 891-2244.

[077] BETHUNE-COOKMAN COLLEGE
ELIGIBILITY: Offers the Lettie Pate Whitehead Foundation Scholarship for Christian females from Virginia, North Carolina, South Carolina, Tennessee, Georgia, Florida, Alabama, Mississippi or Louisiana.
CONTACT: Bethune-Cookman College, 740 Second Avenue, Daytona Beach, FL 02015, (904) 255-1401.

[078] BOARD OF GOVERNOR'S MEDICAL SCHOLARSHIP
ELIGIBILITY: Student must be nominated by the medical school and plan to practice in North Carolina. Financial need required.
AMOUNT: $5,000 +

CONTACT: Financial Aid Office, University of North Carolina, 300 Vance Hall, 057A, Chapel Hill, NC 27599, (919) 962-8396.

---

[079] THE BOSTON CHAPTER OF LINKS, INC.

ELIGIBILITY: Applicants must be black, show financial need, and be from Boston City area. Include with the application a letter of recommendation from a dean and a completed 1040 tax form.
AMOUNT: $1,000
CONTACT: Boston Chapter of Links, Inc., 46 Brockton Street, Mattapan, MA 02126.

---

[080] BOSTON COLLEGE SCHOOL OF EDUCATION

ELIGIBILITY: Graduate school sponsors several fellowships specifically for American minority students who have been accepted into the doctoral programs at Boston College.
AMOUNT: up to $11,000
CONTACT: Arline Riordan, Boston College, Chestnut Hill, MA 02167, (617) 552-4214.

---

[081] BOWDOIN COLLEGE

ELIGIBILITY: John Brown Russwurm Scholarship—all admitted black students; based on academic record and recommendations.
AMOUNT: Varies
CONTACT: Office of Admissions, Bowdoin College, Brunswick, ME 04011, (207) 725-8731.

---

[082] BOWLING GREEN STATE UNIVERSITY

ELIGIBILITY: Black Pioneers Scholarship awarded to black students who excel academically, athletically, or artistically and who demonstrate financial need. Deadline April 1.
AMOUNT: Varies
CONTACT: Bowling Green State University, Attn: Office of Financial Aid, 450 Student Services Bldg., Bowling Green, OH 43403-0145, (419) 372-2651.

[083] BOWLING GREEN STATE UNIVERSITY

ELIGIBILITY: Diversity achievement award for minority students with a minimum 3.25 GPA. Deadline April 1.
AMOUNT: $2,000
CONTACT: Bowling Green State University, Attn: Office of Financial Aid, 450 Student Services Bldg., Bowling Green, OH 43403-0145, (419) 372-2651.

[084] BREAKTHROUGH TO NURSING SCHOLARSHIP

ELIGIBILITY: Minority undergraduate students interested in studying for nursing careers. Financial need a requirement.
AMOUNT: $2,000
CONTACT: National Student Nurses' Association, 10 Columbus Circle, New York, NY 10019, (212) 581-2211.

[085] BRIAR CLIFF COLLEGE MULTICULTURAL SCHOLARSHIPS

ELIGIBILITY: Awards to minority students who have demonstrated leadership. Deadline January 20.
AMOUNT: Half tuition
CONTACT: Briar Cliff College, Attn: Director of Admissions, 3303 Rebecca Street, P.O. Box 2100, Sioux City, IA, 51104-9987, (712) 279-5427.

[086] BUCKNELL UNIVERSITY

ELIGIBILITY: Betty Ann Quinn Fund—available to any black student.
AMOUNT: $400
CONTACT: Office of Admissions, Bucknell University, Lewisburg, PA 17837, (717) 524-1101.

[087] BUCKS COUNTY COMMUNITY COLLEGE

ELIGIBILITY: Minority Incentive Grant. Student must be a U.S. citizen carrying fewer than 6 credits. Subsequent MIG may be awarded for 12 credits. Must have a 2.0 GPA and financial need.

AMOUNT: Tuition and fees
CONTACT: Director of Financial Aid, Bucks County Community College, Swamp Road, Newton, PA 18940, (215) 968-8200.

---

[088] BUSINESS AND PROFESSIONAL WOMEN'S FOUNDATION

ELIGIBILITY: Scholarships for Black Women Over Age 25. Applicants must be black women who are 25 years or older and are pursuing college or other educational courses, seminars, or training opportunities that will enhance their personal or professional skills. Deadline April or September of each year.
AMOUNT: up to $500
CONTACT: Business and Professional Women's Foundation, 2012 Massachusetts Avenue, NW, Washington, DC 20036, (202) 293-1200.

---

[089] CAL GRANT B

ELIGIBILITY: Students who are U.S. citizens and California residents, full-time college students, and in financial need.
AMOUNT: $300 to $5,250
CONTACT: California Student Aid Commission, P.O. Box 942845, Sacramento, CA 94245, (916) 322-6280.

---

[090] CALIFORNIA LIBRARY ASSOCIATION

ELIGIBILITY: Applicants must be pursuing a Master's of Library Science in a California library school. Financial need required. Deadline May 30.
AMOUNT: $2,000
CONTACT: California Library Association, Attn: Scholarship Committee, 717 K Street, Suite 300, Sacramento, CA 95814-3477, (916) 447-8541.

---

[091] CALIFORNIA STATE LIBRARY

ELIGIBILITY: Minority Recruitment. Scholarship is to provide financial assistance to minorities in California who are interested in pursuing

a Master's in Library Science degree. Deadline is June 1.
AMOUNT: $1,500 to $5,000
CONTACT: California State Library, Library Development Services, 1001 6th Street, Suite 300, Sacramento, CA 95814-3324, (916) 323-4400.

---

[092] CALIFORNIA STATE LIBRARY MULTI-ETHNIC SCHOLARSHIP

ELIGIBILITY: Awarded to minority students of California majoring in library science. Deadline June 1.
AMOUNT: $1,000 to $5,000
CONTACT: California State Library, Library Development Services, Attn: Ethnic Services Consultant, P.O. Box 942837, Sacremento, CA 94237-0001, (916) 445-4730.

---

[093] CALIFORNIA STATE UNIVERSITY, DOMINGUEZ HILLS

ELIGIBILITY: TRW Minority Scholarship. The award provides financial assistance to minority students in business administration. Must have a 2.5 GPA.
AMOUNT: Varies
CONTACT: School of Management, California State University, Dominguez Hills, 1000 E. Victoria Street, Carson, CA 90747, (213) 516-3300.

---

[094] CALIFORNIA STATE UNIVERSITY, FULLERTON

ELIGIBILITY: NACME Incentive Awards. Awarded to entering freshman or transfer minorities. Must be a U.S. citizen or permanent resident, have a 2.5 GPA, and major in engineering. Financial need required. Deadline is August 15.
AMOUNT: $250 per year
CONTACT: California State University at Fullerton, 800 N. State College Blvd., Fullerton, CA 92631, (714) 773-2361.

---

[095] CALIFORNIA STATE UNIVERSITY, SACRAMENTO

ELIGIBILITY: KFMT-TV—open to a journalism student from a minority group.
AMOUNT: $300
CONTACT: Office of Admissions, California State University, Sacramento, CA 95819, (916) 454-6723.

[096] CALIFORNIA STATE UNIVERSITY, SACRAMENTO

ELIGIBILITY: Sigma Delta Chi Scholarship—an award for a minority student entering the university to study journalism.
AMOUNT: $100
CONTACT: Office of Admissions, California State University, Sacramento, CA 95819, (916) 454-6723.

[097] CALIFORNIA TEACHERS ASSOCIATION

ELIGIBILITY: The Martin Luther King Jr. Scholarships are available to racial/ethnic minority group CTA members and dependent children of racial/ethnic minority group CTA members in graduate studies. Scholarships vary each year depending on the amount of contributions and the financial need of individual applicants. Applications will be available at CTA Regional Resource Center Offices and the CTA Human Rights Department after January 15. Must be a U.S. citizen. Deadline April 15.
AMOUNT: Varies
CONTACT: Human Rights Dept., California Teachers Assoc., 1705 Murchison Drive, P.O. Box 921, Burlingame, CA 94011-0921, (415) 697-1400.

[098] UNIVERSITY OF CALIFORNIA

ELIGIBILITY: Chancellor's Ethnic Minority Postdoctoral Fellowship Program. Awards made to individuals who show promise for tenure track record at Berkeley. Deadline December 9.
AMOUNT: $31,000 to $35,000
CONTACT: Chancellor's Ethnic Minority Postdoctoral Fellowship

Program, Attn: Office of the Chancellor, 200 California Hall, University of California, Berkeley, Berkeley, CA 94720, (510) 642-1935.

[099] CALIFORNIA UNIVERSITY OF PENNSYLVANIA

ELIGIBILITY: The Board of Governors Minority Scholarship is awarded to 10 minority freshmen. Waives tuition every semester for four years. Must have a 2.5 GPA and a minimum combined SAT score of 725. Deadline April 1.
AMOUNT: Tuition
CONTACT: Admissions Office, California University of Pennsylvania, Third Street, California, PA 15419, (412) 938-4404.

[100] CAL POLYTECH STATE UNIVERSITY

ELIGIBILITY: The War Veterans Scholarship is available to sophomore, junior or senior crop science, animal science or agricultural business management students; preference to disadvantaged minority students. Student aid application for California required. Must have a 3.0 GPA. Deadline March 1.
AMOUNT: Varies
CONTACT: Financial Aid Officer, Cal Polytech State University, Financial Aid Office, San Luis Obispo, CA 93407, (805) 756-1111.

[101] CALVIN THEOLOGICAL SEMINARY

ELIGIBILITY: John H. Kromming Scholarship is available to minority students who reside in North America. The scholarship is applicable to a year of study in any one of the seminary's degree programs. The amount of the scholarship is adjusted to the need of the student and is commensurate with available funds. A recipient may apply for an additional award in a succeeding year. Selection is made on the basis of Christian character, financial need, academic ability, and potential for Christian service. Applicants must be committed to serve in ministry in the Reformed Christian Church. Deadline March 1.
AMOUNT: Varies
CONTACT: Registrar, Calvin Theological Seminary, 3233 Burton Street, SE, Grand Rapids, MI 49506, (616) 957-6036.

[102] CALVIN THEOLOGICAL SEMINARY

ELIGIBILITY: Barney and Martha Bruinsma Memorial Scholarship. Purpose of the scholarship is to promote the ministry of the gospel through North American ethnic minority persons to their own groups. Degree candidates who are preparing to minister primarily to their own groups are eligible. Criteria for selection includes academic ability and achievement, Christian character and commitment, potential for ministry and financial need. Deadline March 1.
AMOUNT: $500
CONTACT: Registrar, Calvin Theological Seminary, 3233 Burton Street, SE, Grand Rapids, MI 49506, (616) 957-6036.

[103] CAPITOL COLLEGE

ELIGIBILITY: The Carl English Scholarship. Applicants will be required to write an essay on careers in engineering technology and must be pursuing an A.A. or B.S. degree. Financial need required. Must be black with a 2.75 GPA. Deadline April 1.
AMOUNT: $1,000 to $2,000
CONTACT: Office of Admissions, Capitol College, 11301 Springfield Road, Laurel, MD 20708, (301) 953-0060.

[104] CARLETON COLLEGE

ELIGIBILITY: Scholarship awards include The Fraser, The Honeywell Fund, and the Minneapolis Star & Tribune Fund for multicultural students entering the college.
AMOUNT: Varies
CONTACT: Carleton College, Office of Admissions, 100 South College Street, Northfield, MN 55057, (507) 663-4190.

[105] CARNEGIE-MELLON UNIVERSITY

ELIGIBILITY: Minority students preparing for careers in insurance, specifically as actuaries.
AMOUNT: Varies
CONTACT: Office of Admissions, Carnegie-Mellon University, 5000 Forbes Avenue, Pittsburgh, PA 15213, (412) 578-2000.

[106] CASE WESTERN RESERVE UNIVERSITY

ELIGIBILITY: Scholarship programs include the Martin Luther King, Jr., Scholarship and the Minority Engineers Industrial Opportunity program.
AMOUNT: $1,000 to $2,000
CONTACT: Office of Admissions, Case Western Reserve University, University Circle, Cleveland, OH 44106, (216) 368-2000.

[107] CASE WESTERN RESERVE UNIVERSITY

ELIGIBILITY: Applicants must have demonstrated ability and achievement. Awarded to U.S. citizens or nationals who are American Indian, Black, Mexican American, Chicano, Puerto Rican, Native Alaskan (Eskimo or Aleut), or Native Pacific Islander (Polynesian or Micronesian) . A 3.0 GPA is required.
AMOUNT: $5,000
CONTACT: Case Western Reserve University, 109 Pardee Hall, Cleveland, OH 44106 , (216) 368-4530.

[108] CASTLETON STATE COLLEGE

ELIGIBILITY: Minority Scholarships Application, FFS/FAF should be submitted to the financial aid office. Financial need required.
AMOUNT: $900 to $2,000
CONTACT: Financial Aid Director, Castleton State College, Castleton, VT 05735, (802) 468-5611.

[109] CATHOLIC NEGRO SCHOLARSHIP FUND

ELIGIBILITY: This fund provides assistance to African Americans pursuing a college education. Applicants must demonstrate need.
AMOUNT: Varies
CONTACT: Catholic Negro Scholarship Fund, 73 Chestnut Street, Springfield, MA 01103.

[110] CENTRAL COLLEGE

ELIGIBILITY: The Multi-Cultural Achievement Scholarship. Three references required, interview requested, and letter of application required. Renewable. Must be an entering minority who is in the upper 3/5 of his/her class and a U.S. citizen. Financial need required. Deadline January 1.
AMOUNT: up to $4,000
CONTACT: Director of Admissions, Central College, 812 University Avenue, Pella, IA 50219, (515) 628-5268.

[111] CENTRAL COLLEGE

ELIGIBILITY: Hearst Scholarship. Leadership potential and communication skills considered. Applicants must rank in the top 10 percent of their class. Renewable with 3.0 GPA. Deadline January 1.
AMOUNT: $5,500
CONTACT: Central College, Attn: Financial Aid Director, 812 University, Pella, IA 50219, (515) 628-5268.

[112] CENTRAL COLLEGE

ELIGIBILITY: McElroy Minority Student Scholarships awarded to a student from the KWWL television viewing area with academic promise, need, and strong moral character. Applicant must rank in the top 10 percent of his or her class. Deadline January 1.
AMOUNT: $5,500
CONTACT: Central College, Attn: Financial Aid Director, 812 University, Pella, IA 50219, (515) 628-5268.

[113] CENTRAL FLORIDA ASSOC. OF BLACKS IN CRIMINAL JUSTICE

ELIGIBILITY: This is provided to black males or females who are criminal justice or political science majors.
AMOUNT: Varies
CONTACT: Central Florida Association, P.O. Box 866, Orlando, FL 32803.

[114] CENTRAL MICHIGAN UNIVERSITY

ELIGIBILITY: Lloyd M. Cofer Scholarship awarded to graduates of public schools in Detroit who show commitment to the advancement of minorities.
AMOUNT: Tuition
CONTACT: Central Michigan University, Attn: Office of Admissions, Mt. Pleasant, MI 48859, (517) 774-3076.

[115] CENTRAL MICHIGAN UNIVERSITY MINORITY ADVANCEMENT SCHOLARSHIP

ELIGIBILITY: Awarded to minority students who show interest in the advancement of minorities in American society. Applicants must be full-time students.
AMOUNT: Varies
CONTACT: Central Michigan University, Attn: Office of Admissions, Mt. Pleasant, MI 48859, (517) 774-3076.

[116] CHARLES DREW SCHOLARSHIP LOAN FUND

ELIGIBILITY: Must be a minority majoring in medicine. Financial need required. Deadline May 30.
AMOUNT: $2,500
CONTACT: Charles Drew Loan Fund, Inc., P.O. Box 431427, Los Angeles, CA 90043.

[117] CHICAGO ASSN. OF BLACK JOURNALISTS SCHOLARSHIPS

ELIGIBILITY: Minority students interested in studying print or broadcast journalism on the undergraduate or graduate level and planning a career in journalism. They must be full-time students in an accredited college or university in the Chicago metro area. Includes northwest Indiana and southern Wisconsin.
AMOUNT: $1,000
CONTACT: Chicago Assn. of Black Journalists, Dept. of Journalism, Northern Illinois University, DeKalb, IL 60115, (815) 753-7017.

[118] CHRISTIAN CHURCH (DISCIPLES OF CHRIST)

ELIGIBILITY: Black Scholarship Fund (Star Supporter) provides black Americans interested in pursuing a career in the ministry of the Christian Church. Applicants must be members of the Christian Church, demonstrate academic ability, have financial need, be enrolled in an accredited postsecondary institution, and submit a transcript of their academic record.

AMOUNT: Varies

CONTACT: Christian Church (Disciples of Christ), 222 South Downey Avenue, P.O. Box 1986, Indianapolis, IN 46206.

[119] CIC MINORITIES FELLOWSHIP, HUMANITIES

ELIGIBILITY: Each award provides full tuition for 4 academic years, plus an annual stipend of $8,500. Fellowship recipients must pursue programs of study leading to Ph.D. degrees and must be accepted as graduate students by at least one of the CIC Universities. Minorities who are U.S. citizens and who hold or will receive a bachelor's degree from a regionally accredited school are eligible. Students who have received a master's degree from a regionally accredited school or students currently enrolled in graduate study may apply. Currently enrolled graduate students at CIC University campuses are not eligible. Must be majoring in: American studies, art history, literature, Germanic literature, linguistics, philosophy, American history, Italian studies, Spanish, romance languages, humanities, Greek/Latin, British literature, German, music theory, religion/theology, French, Portuguese, Slavic studies/languages.

AMOUNT: $8,500 + tuition

CONTACT: Minorities Fellowship Program, Committee on Institutional Cooperation, Kirkwood Hall 114, Indiana University, Bloomington, IN 47405, (800) 457-4420.

[120] CIC MINORITIES FELLOWSHIP, NATURAL SCIENCES

ELIGIBILITY: Each award provides full tuition for 4 academic years plus an annual stipend. Fellowship recipients must pursue programs of study leading to Ph.D. degrees and must be accepted as graduate students by at least one of the CIC Universities. Must be a U.S. citizen who holds

or will receive a bachelor's degree from a regionally accredited school. Students who have received a master's degree from a regionally accredited school or students currently enrolled in graduate study may apply. Currently enrolled graduate students at CIC University campuses are not eligible. Must be majoring in following: agriculture, geology, biology, mathematics, chemistry, physical science, engineering or physics.
AMOUNT: Varies
CONTACT: Committee on Institutional Cooperation, Kirkwood Hall 114, Indiana University, Bloomington, IN 47405, (800) 457-4420.

[121] CIC MINORITIES FELLOWSHIP, SOCIAL SCIENCES

ELIGIBILITY: Each award provides full tuition for 5 academic years, plus an annual stipend of $9,000. Fellowship recipients must pursue programs of study leading to Ph.D. degrees and must be accepted as graduate students by at least one of the CIC Universities. Applicants must be minority students who are U.S. citizens who hold or will receive a bachelor's degree from a regionally accredited school or must have received a master's degree from a regionally accredited school or be currently enrolled in graduate study may apply. Currently enrolled graduate students at CIC University campuses are not eligible. Must be majoring in anthropology, geography, political science, sociology, economics, history or psychology.
AMOUNT: $9,000 + tuition
CONTACT: Minorities Fellowship Program, Committee on Institutional Cooperation, Kirkwood Hall 114, Indiana University, Bloomington, IN 47405, (800) 457-4420.

[122] CIEE EDUCATION ABROAD SCHOLARSHIP FUND FOR MINORITY STUDENTS

ELIGIBILITY: This fund assists minority students who wish to participate in any CIEE educational program including study, work, voluntary service, and internship programs.
AMOUNT: Varies
CONTACT: Council on International Educational Exchange, 205 East 42nd Street, New York, NY 10017, (212) 666-4177.

[123] UNIVERSITY OF CINCINNATI

ELIGIBILITY: Minority Scholars Program. Selection is based on academic performance.
AMOUNT: Varies
CONTACT: Director of Corbett/Minority Scholarships, University of Cincinnati, 300 Tangeman University Center, Cincinnati, OH 45221, (513) 475-8000.

[124] CLARION UNIVERSITY

ELIGIBILITY: The State Board of Governors Scholarships. Amount is based on students' need, and payment is made as a tuition credit. Must have a 3.0 GPA or better and other criteria includes contribution to the university and participation in extracurricular activities.
AMOUNT: Varies
CONTACT: Dean of Admissions, Clarion University, Admissions Office, Clarion, PA 16214, (814) 226-2000.

[125] CLARK ATLANTA UNIVERSITY SCHOOL OF LIBRARY AND INFORMATION STUDIES

ELIGIBILITY: Two library training fellowship grants are provided by the U.S. Dept. of Education. Applicants must be black college seniors majoring in library science. Apply directly to the institution.
AMOUNT: $8,000
CONTACT: Clark Atlanta University, School of Library and Information Studies, 223 James P. Brawley Drive, Atlanta, GA 30314, (404) 653-8694.

[126] CLEMSON UNIVERSITY

ELIGIBILITY: Amoco Foundation Scholarship awarded to a minority or female full-time student in textiles with a 2.0 GPA. Deadline March 1.
AMOUNT: $2,000
CONTACT: Clemson University, Attn: Financial Aid Director, G01 Sikes Hall, Clemson, SC 29634-5123, (803) 656-2280.

[127] CLEMSON UNIVERSITY

ELIGIBILITY: Corinne Holt Sawyer Scholarship awarded to an entering black freshman with a minimum 2.0 GPA. Deadline March 1.
AMOUNT: $1,000
CONTACT: Clemson University, Attn: Financial Aid Director, G01 Sikes Hall, Clemson, SC 29634-5123, (803) 656-2280.

---

[128] CLEMSON UNIVERSITY

ELIGIBILITY: Daniel Memorial Scholarships awarded to minority entering freshmen with a 3.0 GPA. Deadline March 1.
AMOUNT: $1,500
CONTACT: Clemson University, Attn: Financial Aid Director, G01 Sikes Hall, Clemson, SC 29634-5123, (803) 656-2280.

---

[129] CLEMSON UNIVERSITY

ELIGIBILITY: Edward S. Moore Foundation Scholarship awarded to an entering freshman minority student in forestry who is a South Carolina resident. Applicant must have a 3.0 GPA and must be a full-time student. Deadline March 1.
AMOUNT: $2,500 renewable
CONTACT: Clemson University, Attn: Financial Aid Director, G01 Sikes Hall, Clemson, SC 29634-5123, (803) 656-2280.

---

[130] CLEMSON UNIVERSITY

ELIGIBILITY: Harvey B. Gantt Scholarship Endowment Fund. Awards to recruit and retain full-time black students with a 3.0 GPA. Preference to South Carolina residents and entering freshmen. Deadline March 1.
AMOUNT: Varies
CONTACT: Clemson University, Attn: Financial Aid Director, G01 Sikes Hall, Clemson, SC 29634-5123, (803) 656-2280.

---

[131] CLEMSON UNIVERSITY

ELIGIBILITY: Management/Industrial Association Minority Engineering Scholarship. This award is renewable with satisfactory

academic progress.
AMOUNT: $1,000
CONTACT: Financial Aid Director, Clemson University, G01 Sikes Hall, Clemson, SC 29631-4023, (803) 656-2280.

[132] CLEMSON UNIVERSITY

ELIGIBILITY: Robert C. Edwards Scholarships. This renewable award is available to entering freshman with outstanding academic potential. Must have a 2.0 GPA. Deadline is March 1.
AMOUNT: $3,000
CONTACT: Financial Aid Director, Clemson University, G01 Sikes Hall, Clemson, SC 29631-4023, (803) 656-2280.

[133] CLINCH VALLEY COLLEGE

ELIGIBILITY: Black Virginians Scholarships. Applicants must be black students who are residents of Virginia. Selection is based on academic achievement and financial need. Freshmen and transfer students are eligible to apply. A minimum GPA of 2.0 is required. Deadline May 1.
AMOUNT: Varies
CONTACT: Financial Aid Director, Clinch Valley College, P.O. Box 16, Wise, VA 24293, (703) 328-0139.

[134] COALITION OF BLACK MEMBERS OF THE AMERICAN LUTHERAN CHURCH

ELIGIBILITY: One of this organization's goals is to assist black students in their total education in colleges and institutions of the American Lutheran Church.
AMOUNT: Varies
CONTACT: Coalition of Black Members of the American Lutheran Church, 422 So. 5th Street, Minneapolis, MN 55415, (612) 330-3100.

[135] COASTAL CAROLINA COLLEGE

ELIGIBILITY: Admissions Minority Scholarship. Freshman applicants must have a SAT combined score of 800 with a minimum subscore of 400 in verbal and 400 in math or a minimum ACT composite score of 18 with minimum subscores of 18 in English and 18 in Math. Applicants must have been in a college preparatory high school program and be U.S. citizens. Transfer students must have a 3.0 GPA.
AMOUNT: $100
CONTACT: Coastal Carolina College, P.O. Box 1954, Conway, SC 29526, (803) 347-3161.

[136] COE COLLEGE

ELIGIBILITY: Awards available especially for minority students.
AMOUNT: Up to $2,600
CONTACT: Office of Admissions, Coe College, Cedar Rapids, IA 52402, (319) 399-8000.

[137] COLBY COLLEGE

ELIGIBILITY: The Ralph J. Bunche Scholars Program—applicants must show scholastic and leadership potential. Special grants given in addition to usual aid. Amount based on need.
AMOUNT: Varies
CONTACT: Office of Admissions, Colby College, Waterville, ME 04901, (207) 873-1131.

[138] COLLEGE ENTRANCE EXAMINATION BOARD ENGINEERING SCHOLARSHIP PROGRAM FOR MINORITY COMMUNITY COLLEGE GRADUATES

ELIGIBILITY: Scholarships are for minority students who are completing an associate degree to transfer to a four-year college or university in the U.S. to complete study for a bachelor's degree.
AMOUNT: Varies
CONTACT: Engineering Scholarship Program, College Entrance Examination Board, 45 Columbus Avenue, New York, NY 10023-6992, (212) 713-8000.

[139] COLLEGE SCHOLARSHIP SERVICE OF THE COLLEGE BOARD

ELIGIBILITY: Engineering Scholarship Program for Minority Community College Graduates. Individual institutions are invited to nominate minority students for consideration. The nominee should have earned at least a 3.0 GPA; be a U.S. citizen or permanent resident; be scheduled to receive an associate degree or have completed 60 semester hours; have completed calculus, 1 year of general physics, 1 year of general chemistry; demonstrate financial need; and be planning to transfer to an accredited senior institution for full-time study in engineering science.
AMOUNT: Varies
CONTACT: College Scholarship Service of the College Board, 45 Columbus Avenue, New York, NY 10019, (212) 713-8000.

[140] COLORADO COLLEGE

ELIGIBILITY: Award sponsored by the El Pomar Foundation to assist qualified minority students with financial need.
AMOUNT: Varies
CONTACT: Office of Admissions, Colorado College, Colorado Springs, CO 80903, (303) 473-2233 or (800) 542-7214.

[141] COLORADO INSTITUTE OF ART

ELIGIBILITY: Scholarship is open to Colorado minority students. Art work is judged. New program offers first year tuition to winner. One scholarship will be offered each year. Interested students should contact their high school art teacher.
AMOUNT: $7,320
CONTACT: Colorado Institute of Art, Admissions Office, 200 East Ninth Avenue, Denver, CO 80203, (303) 837-0825.

[142] COLORADO SCHOOL OF MINES

ELIGIBILITY: Minority Engineering Scholarship. Applicants must be minorities majoring in one of the following engineering areas; chemical, metallurgy, petroleum, geological or mechanical. Financial need required.

AMOUNT: $250 to $2,500
CONTACT: Financial Aid Director, Colorado School of Mines, Golden, CO 80401, (303) 279-0300.

[143] COLORADO STATE UNIVERSITY
ELIGIBILITY: The Kodak Minority Academic Award is available to a sophomore minority engineering student with a high academic record. Must have a 3.3 GPA. The award pays 75% of tuition and is renewable for three years if the recipient meets the academic standards.
AMOUNT: Varies
CONTACT: Dean of Engineering, Colorado State University, Fort Collins, CO 80523, (303) 491-1101.

[144] COLORADO STATE UNIVERSITY
ELIGIBILITY: For entering freshmen minority students in the College of Agricultural Sciences with financial need, demonstrated scholarship, and leadership. Must be a Colorado resident.
AMOUNT: Varies
CONTACT: Dean of Agricultural Sciences, Colorado State University, Fort Collins, CO 80523, (303) 491-1101.

[145] COLORADO STATE UNIVERSITY
ELIGIBILITY: The Conoco Scholarship is available to outstanding minority students majoring in mechanical or chemical engineering. Must be a U.S. citizen with a 3.3 GPA. Deadline March 1.
AMOUNT: $1,000
CONTACT: Dean of Engineering, Colorado State University, Fort Collins, CO 80523, (303) 491-1101.

[146] COLORADO STATE UNIVERSITY
ELIGIBILITY: Diversity Award. Selection is based on the degree to which a student contributes to the diversity of the environment at the university. The award is renewable if the recipient maintains a minimum 2.0 GPA and the student continues to receive diversity committee approval. Interested students should contact the office of the dean of his/

her academic college or any of the six campus advocacy groups.
AMOUNT: $1,000
CONTACT: Financial Aid Director, Colorado State University, Fort Collins, CO 80523, (303) 491-1101.

---

[147] COLORADO STATE UNIVERSITY
ELIGIBILITY: George and Paula Hill Book Fund. A cash award for materials and expenses available to a minority student pursuing a degree in science. Selection based on financial need. Deadline April 1.
AMOUNT: $100
CONTACT: Vice President, Student Affairs, Colorado State University, Fort Collins, CO 80523, (303) 491-1101.

---

[148] COLORADO STATE UNIVERSITY
ELIGIBILITY: The NACME Scholarship is available to freshmen minority engineering majors. Deadline March 1.
AMOUNT: $500
CONTACT: Dean of Engineering, Colorado State University, Fort Collins, CO 80523, (303) 491-1101.

---

[149] UNIVERSITY OF COLORADO, BOULDER
ELIGIBILITY: Martin Luther King Scholarships. Consideration is automatic and no separate application is required. Deadline March 1.
AMOUNT: Varies
CONTACT: Scholarship Coordinator, University of Colorado at Boulder, Boulder, CO 80309-0106, (303) 492-5091.

---

[150] COLUMBIA INTERNATIONAL UNIVERSITY MINORITY GRANT
ELIGIBILITY: Award to minority full-time students. Deadline February 15.
AMOUNT: $1,200
CONTACT: Columbia International University, Attn: Financial Aid Office, P.O. Box 3122, Columbia, SC 29230-3122, (803) 754-4100.

---

[151] COMMUNITY FOUNDATION OF PALM BEACH/ MARTIN COUNTIES

ELIGIBILITY: Peck Scholarships for a high achiever in French or Spanish pursuing French or Spanish as a major or minor. Applicants must be Palm Beach residents with a minimum 2.5 GPA.
AMOUNT: Varies
CONTACT: Community Foundation of Palm Beach/Martin Counties, Attn: Program Officer, 324 Datura Street, Suite 340, West Palm Beach, FL 33401-5431, (407) 659-6800.

[152] COMMUNITY FOUNDATION OF PALM BEACH/ MARTIN COUNTIES, BARNETT BANK

ELIGIBILITY: Awards to students in good academic standing who intend to major in business. Applicants must be Palm Beach residents with a minimum 2.5 GPA.
AMOUNT: Varies
CONTACT: Community Foundation of Palm Beach/Martin Counties, Attn: Program Officer, 324 Datura Street, Suite 340, West Palm Beach, FL 33401-5431, (407) 659-6800.

[153] CONGRESSIONAL BLACK CAUCUS SPOUSES SCHOLARSHIP

ELIGIBILITY: Applicants must be residents of a congressional district represented by a member of the Congressional Black Caucus in Maryland. Deadline March 25.
AMOUNT: Varies
CONTACT: Congression Black Caucus Foundation, Inc., Attn: Educational Programs Coordinator, 1004 Pennsylvania Avenue, SE, Washington, DC 20003, (202) 675-6730.

[154] UNIVERSITY OF CONNECTICUT

ELIGIBILITY: Medical Scholarship. Must be a minority student majoring in medicine. Financial need required.
AMOUNT: Varies

CONTACT: Financial Aid Director, University of Connecticut, Wilbur Cross Bldg., Storrs, CT 06268, (203) 486-2000.

---

[155] CONSORTIUM FOR GRADUATE STUDY IN MANAGEMENT

ELIGIBILITY: This award is restricted to blacks, Chicanos, Cubans, Native Americans, and Puerto Ricans who wish to attend Indiana University at Bloomington, University of North Carolina at Chapel Hill, University of Rochester, University of Southern California, University of Texas at Austin, Washington University at St. Louis, and the University of Wisconsin at Madison for an MBA. Applicants must be U.S. citizens. Deadline October 1 and February 1.
AMOUNT: Full tuition + expenses
CONTACT: Consortium for Graduate Study in Management, 101 N. Skinker Blvd., P.O. Box 1132, St. Louis, MO 63130, (314) 889-6353.

---

[156] CORGAN ASSOCIATES ARCHITECTS

ELIGIBILITY: African American/Hispanic Architectural Education Work/Study Program. Applicants must be students living within the Dallas Independent School Districts.
AMOUNT: $12,000 total
CONTACT: Gary DeVries, Corgan Associates, Inc., 501 Elm Street, Dallas, TX 75202-3358, (214) 748-2000.

---

[157] CORNELL UNIVERSITY SUMMER COLLEGE

ELIGIBILITY: Jerome H. Holland Scholarship. Applicants must be qualified minority high school juniors and seniors who demonstrate oustanding academic ability as well as financial need.
AMOUNT: Varies
CONTACT: Administrative Assistant, Cornell University Summer College, Box 811, B-12 Ives Hall, Cornell University, Ithaca, NY 14853, (607) 255-6203.

---

[158] COUNCIL ON CAREER DEVELOPMENT FOR MINORITIES JULIUS A THOMAS FELLOWSHIP

ELIGIBILITY: Applicant must be interested in a career in the field of career counseling and placement. In addition to the $2,500 grant, a $150 allowance may be obtained for approved books and materials, and another $2,500 can be earned if student participates in summer internship dealing with counseling and placement. The student must attend one of the following institutions: Florida A&M University (FL), Howard University (DC), North Carolina Central University (NC), Texas Southern University (TX) , Tuskegee Institute (AL), Virginia State University (Petersburg, VA), New Mexico State University (NM), California State University (Long Beach, CA), Pan American University (TX), San Francisco State University (CA). Must be a U.S. citizen. Deadline May 1.
AMOUNT: $2,500
CONTACT: Program Manager, Council on Career Development for Minorities, 1341 W. Mockingbird Lane, Dallas, TX 75247, (214) 631-3677.

[159] COUNCIL ON INTERNATIONAL EDUCATIONAL EXCHANGE

ELIGIBILITY: Robert B. Bailey III Minority Student Scholarship. Applicants must demonstrate financial need and apply to a CIEE-administered study-abroad, work-abroad, or international volunteer work-camp program. Deadline varies.
AMOUNT: $500 - $1,000
CONTACT: Robert B. Bailey III Minority Student Scholarship, Council on International Educational Exchange, 205 East 42nd Street, New York, NY 10017-5706, (212) 666-4177.

[160] COURIER-JOURNAL & THE LOUISVILLE TIMES INTERNSHIP

ELIGIBILITY: The purpose of the minority business intern program is to expose the minority student to newspaper career opportunities. Summer interns are treated as professional staffers and are given opportunities to develop job skills and gain valuable work experience. The program is open to minority college students in their sophomore or junior years who

either live or go to college in Kentucky or Southern Indiana. Children of employees are eligible but receive no preferential treatment. The participating departments and number of positions vary from year to year. The internship lasts 13 weeks. Interns will work a full work week. Days off will not necessarily be on weekends. Interns earn $200 a week. A business resume and cover letter must be submitted with the official application form. Must be majoring in photojournalism, accounting, advertising, journalism, business administration/management, or engineering. Deadline March 31.
AMOUNT: Varies
CONTACT: Human Resources Dept., The Courier-Journal & The Louisville Times, 525 West Broadway, Louisville, KY 40202, (502) 582-4803.

---

[161] COX NEWSPAPERS MINORITY JOURNALISM SCHOLARSHIP
ELIGIBILITY: Scholarship includes 4 years paid internship and a position at Cox Newspapers upon graduation. Must have a 3.0 GPA. Deadline April 1.
AMOUNT: Tuition and fees
CONTACT: Scholarship Officer, Cox Enterprises, P.O. Box 4689, Atlanta, GA 30302, (404) 526-5091.

---

[162] CREIGHTON UNIVERSITY
ELIGIBILITY: Black Undergraduate Scholarship. Applicants must maintain a 2.5 GPA and prove financial need.
AMOUNT: Tuition, room and board
CONTACT: Financial Aid Office, Creighton University, California at 24th Street, Omaha, NE 68178, (402) 280-2731.

---

[163] CREOLE ETHNIC ASSOCIATION, INC.
ELIGIBILITY: Creole Scholarship Fund provides financial services to undergraduate or graduate students conducting research in the areas of genealogy, language, or Creole culture. Applicants must be U.S. citizens and are asked to fill out a genealogical chart of at least five generations.

Deadline June.
AMOUNT: $1,000
CONTACT: Creole Ethnic Association, Inc., P.O. Box 2666, Church Street Station, New York, NY 10008.

[164] DAILY PRESS SCHOLARSHIPS FOR BLACK JOURNALISTS

ELIGIBILITY: Black students either interested in studying print journalism or already in print journalism. Preference given to residents of the Virginia Peninsula.
AMOUNT: $2,500
CONTACT: Daily Press, Inc., 7505 Warwick Blvd., P.O. Box 746, Newport News, VA 23607, (804) 244-8421.

[165] DALLAS-FORT WORTH ASSOCIATION OF BLACK COMMUNICATORS

ELIGIBILITY: Applicants must be black entering freshman and must reside in Dallas, Tarrant, Collin or Denton County. Must be majoring in one of the following: journalism, photojournalism, public relations, radio/TV broadcasting or graphic arts.
AMOUNT: $1,500
CONTACT: DFW/ABC, 400 Records Street, Belo Bldg., Suite 343, Dallas, TX 75265.

[166] DARTMOUTH COLLEGE

ELIGIBILITY: Thurgood Marshall Dissertation Fellowships for African American Scholars. Applicants must have completed all other Ph.D. requirements other than the disseration at Dartmouth College. Each fellow will be expected to complete the disseration during the tenure of the fellowship and to participate in teaching one ten-week course during the year. Deadline March 1.
AMOUNT: $20,000+
CONTACT: Office of the Dean of the Faculty, Dartmouth College, 201 Wentworth Hall, Hanover, NH 03755, (603) 646-1110.

[167] DEFIANCE COLLEGE
ELIGIBILITY: Awards to minority students graduating in the top 50% of their high school class.
AMOUNT: $1,500
CONTACT: Defiance College, Attn: Office of Financial Aid, 701 North Clinton Street, Defiance, OH 43512, (419) 783-2355.

[168] DELAWARE VALLEY CLUB SCHOLARSHIP
ELIGIBILITY: To a minority high school senior Delaware Valley resident who has interest in service to the community. Must have a 3.0 GPA and financial need. Deadline May 23.
AMOUNT: $750
CONTACT: Scholarship Chairperson, Delaware Valley Club, 2324 47th Street, Pennsauken, NJ 08110, (609) 662-8739.

[169] DELTA SIGMA THETA, INC.
ELIGIBILITY: Myra Davis Hemmings Scholarship. Applicants must be active, dues-paying members of Delta Sigma Theta and majoring in the performing or creative arts. Applicants must submit transcripts of all college records. Deadline March.
AMOUNT: Varies
CONTACT: Delta Sigma Theta, Inc., 1707 New Hampshire Avenue, NW, Washington, DC 20009, (202) 483-5460.

[170] DELTA SIGMA THETA SORORITY
ELIGIBILITY: Scholarships for women from Montgomery or Prince George's counties in Maryland for study at either a college or specialized vocational school.
AMOUNT: Varies
CONTACT: Delta Sigma Theta Sorority, Inc., 1707 New Hampshire Avenue, NW, Washington, DC 20009, (202) 483-5460.

[171] DELTA SIGMA THETA SORORITY

ELIGIBILITY: Potomac Valley Alumnae Chapter. Scholarships for residents of Montgomery County in Maryland who demonstrate financial need. Deadline March 31.

AMOUNT: $2,000

CONTACT: Potomac Valley Alumnae Chapter, Delta Sigma Theta Sorority, Inc., Attn: Scholarship Committee, 9913 Sorrel Avenue, Potomac, MD 20854, (301) 299-8011.

[172] DENISON UNIVERSITY

ELIGIBILITY: Denison University offers 41 minority student scholarships as follows: 17 Tyree Scholarships, 9 Meredity Scholarships, 12 Fisher Scholarships, and 3 Bob Good Scholarships.

AMOUNT: range from $1,500 to $2,500

CONTACT: Financial Aid Director, Denison University, Granville, OH 43023, (614) 587-0810.

[173] DENISON UNIVERSITY PARAJON SCHOLARSHIP

ELIGIBILITY: Awarded to Hispanic, Asian, and Native American students who show outstanding academic performance or potential. Deadline January 1.

AMOUNT: Half tuition

CONTACT: Denison University, Attn: Financial Aid Director, Office of Financial Aid and Student Employment, Box H, Granville, OH 43023, (614) 587-6279.

[174] DEPAUW UNIVERSITY

ELIGIBILITY: Applicant must be a black U.S. citizen and possess leadership qualities. Deadline February 15.

AMOUNT: $5,000

CONTACT: Depauw University, 309 S. Locust Street, Administration Bldg., Greencastle, IN 46135, (317) 658-4030.

[175] DIGITAL EQUIPMENT CORPORATION

ELIGIBILITY: Offers a minority education scholarship for students majoring in electrical, mechanical, or industrial engineering or computer science in their last two years of college.
AMOUNT: Varies
CONTACT: Digital Equipment Corporation, 2500 West Union Hills Drive, Phoenix, AZ 85027.

[176] DIGITAL EQUIPMENT CORP. MINORITIES AND WOMEN ENGINEERS

ELIGIBILITY: Minority and women high school juniors and seniors who are residents of Springfield, W. Springfield, Holyoke, Chicopee, Agawam or Westfield, or are children of Digital Equipment Corp./ Springfield employees, regardless of their place of residence are eligible; Recipients will be invited work at Digital/Springfield during the summer. Scholarship support may be extended beyond freshman year if student performs acceptably during summer work program and during college year. Must major in engineering. Financial need required. Deadline February 2.
AMOUNT: Tuition + fees
CONTACT: Digital Equipment Corporation, 2500 West Union Hills Drive, Phoenix, AZ 85027.

[177] DOW JONES NEWSPAPER FUND

ELIGIBILITY: Minority Editing Intern Program for College Seniors. This newspaper intern program offers minority college seniors a paid summer copy-editing internship on daily newspapers and a scholarship to use for graduate studies following the internship or a grant to pay outstanding school loans. Deadline November 15.
AMOUNT: Paid internship + $1,000 grant
CONTACT: Dow Jones Newspaper Fund, Inc., P.O. Box 300, Princeton, NJ 08543-0300.

[178] DR. MARTIN LUTHER KING, JR., MEMORIAL SCHOLARSHIP AWARD

ELIGIBILITY: Black high school graduates are eligible. Winners determined by SAT scores, GPA, leadership, recommendations and personal interviews.
AMOUNT: $2,000
CONTACT: Educational and Cultural Fund of the Electrical Industry, Electric Industry Center, 158-11 Jewel Avenue, Flushing, NY 11365.

[179] DRAKE UNIVERSITY COWLES FOUNDATION MULTICULTURAL SCHOLARSHIP

ELIGIBILITY: Award available to minority full-time students with a minimum 3.75 GPA, combined 1210 SAT score, minimum 27 ACT score, and who are in the top 1/5 of their high school class. Deadline March 1.
AMOUNT: Tuition
CONTACT: Drake University, Attn: Director of Admissions, Des Moines, IA 50311-4505, (515) 271-3181.

[180] DREXEL UNIVERSITY

ELIGIBILITY: Business Minority Award. Four-year Malcolm X Scholarship provides tuition, books, fees, and room and board.
AMOUNT: Varies
CONTACT: Office of Admissions, Drexel University, Philadelphia, PA 19104, (215) 895-2400.

[181] DUKE UNIVERSITY

ELIGIBILITY: Award sponsored by the Gulf Oil Corporation Foundation. Scholarships are available for minority students interested in engineering and science who are in financial need.
AMOUNT: Up to $2,000
CONTACT: Office of Admissions, Duke University, Durham, NC 27708, (919) 684-3214.

[182] DUKE UNIVERSITY

ELIGIBILITY: Reginaldo Howard Memorial Scholarship. Selection is based on academic ability and leadership skills. These awards are renewable. Applicants must be in the upper 1/5 of their class and have a 3.3 GPA.
AMOUNT: $6,000
CONTACT: Director of Admissions, Duke University, Durham, NC 27708, (919) 684-3214.

[183] DURACELL/NATIONAL URBAN LEAGUE SCHOLARSHIP & INTERN PROGRAM

ELIGIBILITY: Applicants must be in the upper 25% of their class majoring in one of the following: marketing, finance, engineering, business administration/management, sales. Deadline April 15.
AMOUNT: $10,000 and summer internships
CONTACT: The Duracell/National Urban League, 500 East 62nd Street, New York, NY 10021-8309, (212) 310-9000.

[184] DURHAM TECHNICAL INSTITUTE SCHOLARSHIP PROGRAM

ELIGIBILITY: In order to qualify, a student must maintain a passing grade average at or above the level for graduation. Preference will be given to those with the greatest need, minority, black students enrolled in college transferable curriculum programs, displaced persons seeking new job skills, and women in nontraditional curriculum programs (in that order). Other factors to be considered will include scholastic achievement and participation in institution and community activities. Deadline varies.
AMOUNT: $400
CONTACT: Financial Aid Director, Durham Technical Institute, 1637 Lawson Street, Durham, NC 27703, (919) 596-9311.

[185] EARL WARREN LEGAL TRAINING PROGRAM

ELIGIBILITY: Preference will be given to students enrolling in law schools in the South. Applicants must take the law school admissions test. Consideration is given to applicants under 35 years of age and to those who plan to practice where there is a great need for lawyers. Must be a

black U.S. citizen.
AMOUNT: $1,200
CONTACT: Earl Warren Legal Training Program, 99 Hudson Street, Suite 1600, New York, NY 10013, (212) 219-1900.

---

[186] EARLHAM COLLEGE
ELIGIBILITY: Awards the Educational Enhancement Awards to Indiana black and Hispanic students enrolling at Earlham. The grants are based on demonstrated financial need. Grants include a guaranteed campus job, allowing qualified students to earn a four-year Earlham degree without incurring any debt.
CONTACT: Robert L. De Veer, Dean of Admissions, Earlham College, Richmond, IN 47374, (317) 983-1600 or toll free (800) 382-6906.

---

[187] EARLHAM COLLEGE
ELIGIBILITY: The Cunningham Cultural Scholarship. Must submit a recommendation from a teacher and be willing to attend April Scholar's forum. Deadline is March 1.
AMOUNT: $2,500 to $4,000
CONTACT: Earlham College, Office of Admissions, Richmond, IN 47374, (317) 983-1600.

---

[188] EAST TENNESSEE STATE UNIVERSITY MINORITY SCHOLARSHIP
ELIGIBILITY: Awarded to minority students.
AMOUNT: $950
CONTACT: East Tennessee State University, Attn: Office of Financial Aid, P.O. Box 70722, Johnson City, TN 37614-0722, (615) 929-4313.

---

[189] EAST TEXAS STATE UNIVERSITY
ELIGIBILITY: The Harvey Martin Scholarship is available to minority high school or college students who exhibit leadership and scholarship ability. Students must be in the upper quarter of their high school class or possess a 3.0 GPA in college work. A letter requesting consideration must

be submitted to the office of special services. Deadline July 5.
AMOUNT: $200
CONTACT: Office of Special Services, East Texas State University, Commerce, TX 75428, (214) 886-5014.

---

[190] EAST TEXAS STATE UNIVERSITY
ELIGIBILITY: The Placid Oil Company Scholarship is for an accounting major who is a minority student (females considered minority) with a 3.0 GPA, who is active in extracurricular activities and has financial need. No application is required.
AMOUNT: $500
CONTACT: Accounting Dept., East Texas State University, Commerce, TX 75428, (214) 886-5014.

---

[191] EAST TEXAS STATE UNIVERSITY
ELIGIBILITY: The United Minority Student Scholarship is for entering freshmen and transfer minority students who are in the upper quarter of their high school class with a 3.25 GPA or transfer students with a 3.0 GPA on a 4.0 system. Students are sought for their leadership and scholarly abilities.
AMOUNT: $200
CONTACT: Office of Special Services, East Texas State University, Commerce, TX 75428, (214) 886-5014.

---

[192] EASTERN COLLEGE
ELIGIBILITY: Applicants must be in the upper 2/5 of their class with a 2.3 GPA. Awarded on a first-come, first-serve basis.
AMOUNT: $1,000 to $5,000
CONTACT: Eastern College, Minority Student Recruitment, St. Davids, PA 31908, (215) 341-1376.

---

[193] EASTERN MENNONITE COLLEGE
ELIGIBILITY: American Minority Scholarship. Two scholarships are available to American minority students who have maintained a satisfactory record at Eastern Mennonite College. Applicants are required to

submit a statement of service goals and demonstrate financial need. Deadline March 1.
AMOUNT: $450
CONTACT: Financial Aid Director, Eastern Mennonite College, Harrisonburg, VA 22801, (703) 433-2771.

---

[194] EDGES GROUP SCHOLARSHIP PROGRAM

ELIGIBILITY: This program provides assistance to black students who are planning to major in business. Applicants who live in New York, New Jersey, or Connecticut are eligible if they meet the educational and economic criteria established by the United Negro College Fund and are interested in attending a UNCF-affiliated school.
AMOUNT: $4,000 renewable
CONTACT: EDGES Group, Inc., c/o William H. Blakely, Jr., 1221 Avenue of the Americas, New York, NY 10020, (212) 790-6058.

---

[195] EDUCATIONAL OPPORTUNITY FUND GRANTS

ELIGIBILITY: Applicants must be from educationally disadvantaged backgrounds, be able to show financial need, be residents of New Jersey, and be enrolled in a New Jersey college or university.
AMOUNT: $200 to $1,200
CONTACT: New Jersey Department of Higher Education, P.O. Box 1417, Trenton, NJ 08625, (609) 292-4368.

---

[196] ELKS NATIONAL FOUNDATION SCHOLARSHIP

ELIGIBILITY: High school seniors who show leadership, outstanding academic performance, and financial need. Must live within the jurisdictions of the Elks.
AMOUNT: $1,000 to $5,000
CONTACT: Improved Benevolent Protective Order of Elks of the World, P.O. Box 159, Winton, NC 29786, (919) 358-7661.

---

[197] EMERSON COLLEGE

ELIGIBILITY: WCVB-TV Scholarship is available to a junior, senior, or graduate student in broadcast journalism who is considered disadvan-

taged. Preference is given to black, Spanish, Hispanic, Asian, or American Indian students. The recipient must be an American citizen or satisfactorily demonstrate that he/she plans to remain in the U.S. for his/her life work. Must have a 3.0 GPA and financial need required. Deadline April 1.
AMOUNT: $1,250
CONTACT: Financial Aid Director, Emerson College, 100 Beacon Street, Boston, MA 02116, (617) 578-8655.

[198] EMORY UNIVERSITY
ELIGIBILITY: Martin Luther King Scholarship. The applicant must demonstrate qualities of mind and spirit and academic and personal achievements that would honor the memory of the late civil rights leader. Must be in the upper 1/5 of their class and be an entering black freshman. Deadline December 1.
AMOUNT: Varies
CONTACT: Emory University, 1380 Oxford Road, NE, Atlanta, GA 30322-1018, (404) 727-6036.

[199] ENVIRONMENTAL PROTECTION AGENCY
ELIGIBILITY: Minority Institution Assistance Fellowships are available to any minority full-time undergraduates pursuing environmental careers at historically black colleges/universities. Applicants must apply two years before receiving a BS degree and have a cumulative 3.0 GPA.
AMOUNT: Full tuition+
CONTACT: Minority Institution Assistance Fellowships, Environmental Protection Agency, Office of Exploratory Research, Mail Stop 8703, 401 M Street, SW, Washington, DC 20460, (202) 260-5750.

[200] EQUAL OPPORTUNITY PUBLICATIONS SCHOLARSHIP PROGRAM
ELIGIBILITY: Must be a full-time student working toward a bachelor's degree in any engineering discipline. Selection based on GPA, extracurricular activities, a personal statement, and a recommendation. Females only. Deadline February 15.

AMOUNT: $500
CONTACT: Career Opportunities Through Education, P.O. Box 2810, Cherry Hill, NJ 08034, (609) 795-9634.

---

[201] UNIVERSITY OF EVANSVILLE
ELIGIBILITY: The Martin Luther King Scholarship is intended to assist minority students showing academic promise and pursuing a professional career. Deadline March 1.
AMOUNT: Varies
CONTACT: Financial Aid Director, University of Evansville, 1800 Lincoln Avenue, Evansville, IN 47722, (812) 479-2364.

---

[202] FAYETTEVILLE STATE UNIVERSITY ACADEMIC SCHOLARSHIP PROGRAM
ELIGIBILITY: Awards for all majors but especially for band, choir, art, drama, or athletics.
AMOUNT: $4,200 renewable
CONTACT: Mr. Charles Darlington, Director, Enrollment Management and Admissions, Fayetteville State University, 1200 Murchison Road, Fayetteville, NC 28301-4298, (919) 486-1371.

---

[203] FISK UNIVERSITY
ELIGIBILITY: The number of awards vary. Must be a black college freshman. Must have a strong academic background. Apply early.
AMOUNT: $100 to $2,000
CONTACT: Fisk University, 1000 17th Avenue, North, Nashville, TN 37208-3051, (615) 329-8665.

---

[204] FIVE COLLEGE FELLOWSHIP PROGRAM FOR MINORITY SCHOLARS
ELIGIBILITY: The Five College Fellowship Program brings to the Five Colleges minority graduate students who have completed all requirements for the Ph.D. except the dissertation. Deadline January 15.
AMOUNT: $20,000

CONTACT: Lorna M. Peterson, Five College Fellowship Program Committee, Five Colleges, Inc., P.O. Box 740, Amherst, MA 01004, (413) 256-3626.

[205] FLORIDA A&M UNIVERSITY
ELIGIBILITY: Life Gets Better Scholarship.
AMOUNT: $10,000 renewable
CONTACT: Deborah Hardy, Florida A&M University, Tallahassee, FL 32307, (904) 599-3225.

[206] FLORIDA ATLANTIC UNIVERSITY
ELIGIBILITY: Martin Luther King Scholarships available to incoming black freshmen in the upper 1/5 of their class. Deadline March 1.
AMOUNT: Varies
CONTACT: Florida Atlantic University, Attn: Office of Admissions, 500 NW 20th Street, Boca Raton, FL 33431-0991, (407) 367-3000.

[207] FLORIDA ATLANTIC UNIVERSITY
ELIGIBILITY: Minority transfer scholarships are available to incoming black juniors who have at least a 3.0 GPA. Deadline is March 1.
AMOUNT: $775
CONTACT: Financial Aid Director, Florida Atlantic University, Student Services Bldg., Room 227, Boca Raton, FL 33431-0991, (407) 367-3000.

[208] FLORIDA ATLANTIC UNIVERSITY
ELIGIBILITY: The Minority Educational Awards are available to encourage academic excellence and leadership among black students who matriculate at the university in graduate programs. Contact the dean of the college of enrollment for additional information.
AMOUNT: Varies
CONTACT: Florida Atlantic University, Student Services Building, Room 227, Boca Raton, FL 33431-0991, (407) 367-3000.

[209] FLORIDA ATLANTIC UNIVERSITY

ELIGIBILITY: The Black Student Union Scholarship is available to minority students entering their junior year. Applicants must demonstrate financial need and maintain a minimum 2.5 GPA. Financial need required.
AMOUNT: $100
CONTACT: Florida Atlantic University, Student Services Bldg., Room 227, Boca Raton, FL 33431-0991, (407) 367-3000.

[210] FLORIDA ATLANTIC UNIVERSITY

ELIGIBILITY: Emily B. and Robert Murdick Scholarship awarded to a full-time black student with a 3.0 GPA and who demonstrates financial need. Deadline July 1.
AMOUNT: $5,000
CONTACT: Florida Atlantic University, Attn: Financial Aid Office, 500 NW 20th Street, Bacon Raton, FL 33431-0991, (407) 367-3530.

[211] FLORIDA ATLANTIC UNIVERSITY

ELIGIBILITY: The North Broward Hospital Scholarships are available to minority or female students from Broward County majoring in health administration. Selection is based on academic achievement and financial need. Must have a 3.0 GPA and show financial need. Deadline March 1.
AMOUNT: Varies
CONTACT: Health Administration Program, Florida Atlantic University, Boca Raton, FL 33431, (407) 367-3000.

[212] FLORIDA COMMUNITY COLLEGE AT JACKSONVILLE

ELIGIBILITY: Black Student Grant for incoming freshmen enrolling full-time. Applicants must be a U.S. citizen. Deadline February 28.
AMOUNT: $1,150
CONTACT: Florida Community College at Jacksonville, Attn: Scholarship Coordinator, 501 West State Street, Jacksonville, FL 32202, (904) 632-3353.

[213] FLORIDA DEPARTMENT OF EDUCATION

ELIGIBILITY: Jose Marti Scholarship Challenge Grant Fund. Awards offered to Hispanic Florida residents beginning undergraduate or graduate studies at a Florida college. Applicants must apply as a senior in high school or as a graduate student with a 3.0 GPA. Applicant must be a U.S. citizen. Deadline April 1.

AMOUNT: $2,000

CONTACT: Florida Department of Education, Assistance-State Programs, Attn: Office of Student Financial Assistance, 1344 Florida Education Center, Tallahassee, FL 32399-0400, (904) 487-0049.

[214] FLORIDA INSTITUTE OF TECHNOLOGY

ELIGIBILITY: Minority Engineering Education Effort. Applicants must be full-time students with a 2.5 GPA, majoring in engineering. Financial need required. Deadline May 1.

AMOUNT: $1,500

CONTACT: Engineering Department, Florida Institute of Technology, Office of Financial Aid/Scholarships, 150 W. University Blvd., Melbourne, FL 32901, (407) 768-8000.

[215] FLORIDA INTERNATIONAL UNIVERSITY

ELIGIBILITY: Academic Opportunity Program for incoming freshmen with a minimum GPA of 3.0, a combined SAT score of 850, and a record of school and community involvement. Deadline December 1.

AMOUNT: $1,200

CONTACT: Florida International University, Attn: Director of Minority Student Services, University Park Campus, GC 216, Miami, FL 33199, (305) 348-2436.

[216] FLORIDA INTERATIONAL UNIVERSITY

ELIGIBILITY: CRC Press Scholarship for full-time minority students with a minimum GPA of 3.0, demonstrating financial need, and majoring in English, communications, marketing, sales, retailing, or accounting. Deadline May 1.

AMOUNT: $1,500

CONTACT: Florida International University, Attn: Office of Financial Aid, University Park Campus, PC 125, Miami, FL 33199, (305) 348-2436.

---

[217] FLORIDA INTERNATIONAL UNIVERSITY
ELIGIBILITY: Golden Drum Scholarship for incoming black freshmen with a minimum GPA of 3.0, a combined SAT score of 900, ACT score of 25, and a record of school and community involvement. Deadline December 17.
AMOUNT: $1,200
CONTACT: Florida International University, Attn: Director of Minority Student Services, University Park Campus, GC 216, Miami, FL 33199, (305) 348-2436.

---

[218] FLORIDA INTERNATIONAL UNIVERSITY
ELIGIBILITY: The Sarah and Solomon Rosenberg Scholarship is available to black juniors or seniors who are majoring in engineering, computer science or business. Applicants must show financial need. Deadline is July 1.
AMOUNT: Varies
CONTACT: Financial Aid Director , Florida International University, Tamiami Trail, Miami, FL 33199, (305) 554-2431.

---

[219] FLORIDA MEMORIAL COLLEGE
ELIGIBILITY: Applicants must be a black entering freshman with a strong academic background. Apply early.
AMOUNT: $100 to $2,000
CONTACT: Florida Memorial College, 15800 NW 42nd Street, Miami, FL 33054, (305) 625-4141.

---

[220] FLORIDA SOCIETY OF NEWSPAPER EDITORS
JOURNALISM SCHOLARSHIP
ELIGIBILITY: Award is for minority senior journalism students attending a Florida College or University.

AMOUNT: $2,000
CONTACT: Managing Editor, Florida Society of Newspaper Editors, The Tampa Tribune, 202 Parkway Street, Tampa, FL 33606.

---

[221] FLORIDA STATE UNIVERSITY AND THE UNIVERSITY OF FLORIDA LAW SCHOOLS

ELIGIBILITY: The Virgil Hawkins Fellowship is for minority students enrolled full time at FSU and the University of Florida Law Schools. Awards are given yearly for a maximum of three years.
AMOUNT: $5,000
CONTACT: Florida State University, Attn: Dean of Law School, 425 West Jefferson Street, Tallahassee, FL 32306-1034, (904) 644-7338.

---

[222] UNIVERSITY OF FLORIDA

ELIGIBILITY: The New York Times Scholarship—open to either a graduate or undergraduate student in the field of journalism. Priority given to minority group members.
AMOUNT: $750 to $1,500
CONTACT: Office of Admissions, University of Florida, 233 Tigert Hall, Gainesville, FL 32611, (904) 392-3261.

---

[223] UNIVERSITY OF FLORIDA LAW SCHOOL VIRGIL HAWKINS FELLOWSHIP

ELIGIBILITY: Fellowships for minority students attending University of Florida Law Schools.
AMOUNT: $5,000
CONTACT: Hawkins Fellowship Administration, Dept. of Education, Office of Student Financial Assistant, University of Florida, Tallahassee, FL 32399.

---

[224] FORD FOUNDATION POSTDOCTORAL FELLOWSHIPS FOR MINORITIES

ELIGIBILITY: Must be planning a career in teaching/education. Deadline January 13.

AMOUNT: Varies
CONTACT: National Research Council Office, Fellowship Office, HR 420A, 2101 Constitution Avenue, NW, Washington, DC 20418, (202) 334-2000.

[225] FOUNDATION FOR EXCEPTIONAL CHILDREN SCHOLARSHIPS

ELIGIBILITY: For disabled, disabled minority, disabled gifted or disabled gifted minority students with financial need. Deadline February 1.
AMOUNT: Varies
CONTACT: Scholarship Committee, Foundation for Exceptional Children, 1920 Association Drive, Reston, VA 22091, (703) 620-1054.

[226] FRANKLIN AND MARSHALL COLLEGE

ELIGIBILITY: William Gray Scholarships awarded to minority students selected on academic ability, leadership, and strong moral character.
AMOUNT: Tuition+
CONTACT: Franklin and Marshall College, Admissions Office, P.O. Box 3003, Lancaster, PA 17604-3003, (717) 291-3951.

[227] FRIENDS UNIVERSITY

ELIGIBILITY: J. David Jackson Scholarship is available to minority students with first preference given to Native American students.
AMOUNT: Varies
CONTACT: Financial Aid Director, Friends University, 2100 University, Wichita, KS 67213, (316) 261-5887.

[228] FUND FOR THEOLOGICAL EDUCATION

ELIGIBILITY: Candidates must be black citizens of the U.S. or Canada and official candidates for ministerial ordination within their communion. All nominees must be prepared to enroll in a master of divinity program at a theological school that is fully accredited with the association of theological schools in the U.S. and Canada in the autumn following

receipt of the award. No midyear fellowships are awarded. Stipends will vary in amount according to need. The awards are not intended to replace financial aid normally offered by institutions where the recipient is studying. Fellowships are awarded on the basis of competence and promise, not financial need. Renewals are contingent upon each fellow maintaining a high academic record as well as other evidence of promise for ministerial effectiveness. Each individual must be nominated by a minister, member of the faculty or administration, or a former fellow of programs administered by the fund. The letter of nomination should provide the name and current address of the nominee and must be received no later than November 20 of each year.
AMOUNT: Varies
CONTACT: Fund for Theological Education, 421 Wall Street, Research Park, Princeton, NJ 08540, (609) 924-0004.

---

[229] GARDEN CITY COMMUNITY COLLEGE
ELIGIBILITY: Angie Gonzales Posey Memorial Scholarship applicants must be a minorities with a 2.5 GPA. Nonrenewable.
AMOUNT: $200
CONTACT: Dean of Student Services, Garden City Community College, Lulac Education Center, 801 Campus Drive, Garden City, KS 67846, (316) 276-7611.

---

[230] GE FOUNDATION ENGINEERING AND BUSINESS ADMINISTRATION SCHOLARSHIP PROGRAMS
ELIGIBILITY: High achieving minority students enrolled in a transfer program at two-year colleges with a 3.0 GPA or higher. Applicants must be nominated by college/school official and complete the application procedures. Deadline November 15.
AMOUNT: Varies
CONTACT: Barbara Kram, Grant Program for Minority Engineering and Business Students, The College Board, 45 Columbus Avenue, New York, NY 10023-6992, (212) 713-8000.

---

[231] GEORGE FOX COLLEGE MINORITY AWARDS
ELIGIBILITY: Awarded to minority students.
AMOUNT: $1,000 to $2,500
CONTACT: George Fox College, Attn: Financial Aid Office, 414 N. Meridian Street, Newberg, OR 97132-2625, (503) 538-8383.

[232] GEORGE E. JOHNSON FOUNDATION AND EDUCATIONAL FUND
ELIGIBILITY: Applicant must be a minority student, a citizen of the U.S., already accepted as a full-time student in an accredited four-year institution, and demonstrate financial need. Applicants must be studying business administration, engineering, chemistry, physics, pre-dentistry, or pre-law.
AMOUNT: Varies
CONTACT: Clotte Y. Best, Assistant Administrator, Johnson Products Co., Inc., 8522 South Lafayette Avenue, Chicago, IL 60620-1301, (312) 483-4100.

[233] GEORGE WASHINGTON CARVER SCHOLARSHIP
ELIGIBILITY: Minority students graduating from select high schools in Santa Barbara, California, with a 2.5 GPA and in financial need.
AMOUNT: Varies
CONTACT: George Washington Carver Scholarship Club, Inc., c/o Mrs. William E. King, 626-B East De LaGuerra, Santa Barbara, CA 93103.

[234] GEORGETOWN UNIVERSITY
ELIGIBILITY: Aid is available through Law Center Minority Scholarship Funds.
AMOUNT: Varies
CONTACT: Office of Admissions, Georgetown University, 37th & 0 Streets, NW, Washington, D.C. 20057, (202) 625-0100.

[235] GMI ENGINEERING/MANAGEMENT INSTITUTE

ELIGIBILITY: NACME Scholarship. Applicants must be minority U.S. citizens or permanent residents. May be an incoming freshman or transfer student. Award is based on need and/or merit and is renewable for up to 4 1/2 years. Financial need required. Deadline April 15.
AMOUNT: $250 to 1,000
CONTACT: Director of Financial Aid, GMI/Engineering/Management Institute, 1700 W. Third Avenue, Room 2-328CC, Flint, MI 48504-4898, (800) 521-7436.

[236] GOLDEN STATE MINORITY FOUNDATION, FINANCIAL AID

ELIGIBILITY: This scholarship is available to residents of or attending school in southern California. Students must be full-time and must work no more than 25 hours per week. Must have a 3.0 GPA and major in business administration/management. Deadline October 1 for northern California and March1 for southern California.
AMOUNT: $2,000
CONTACT: Scholarship Officer, Golden State Minority Foundation, 1999 W. Adams Blvd., Los Angeles, CA 90018, (213) 731-7771.

[237] GOLDEN STATE MINORITY SCHOLARSHIPS

ELIGIBILITY: Qualified minority students accepted to or enrolled in a college or university in an area where the foundation conducts fund-raising.
AMOUNT: Varies
CONTACT: Golden State Minority Foundation, 1999 W. Adams Blvd., Los Angeles, CA 90018, (213) 731-7771.

[238] GOLUB FOUNDATION

ELIGIBILITY: Tillie Golub-Schwartz Memorial Scholarship. Awarded to a full-time minority student attending a four-year school in Vermont, New York, Pennsylvania, or Massachusetts. Deadline March 15.
AMOUNT: $8,000

CONTACT: Golub Foundation, Attn: Scholarship Committee, P.O. Box 1074, Schenectady, NY 12301, (518) 356-9375.

[239] GOSHEN COLLEGE MULTICULTURAL LEADERSHIP SCHOLARSHIP

ELIGIBILITY: Awarded to a minority student entering college with a minimum 2.5 GPA and in the upper 2/5 of the graduating class.
AMOUNT: $1,000
CONTACT: Goshen College, Attn: Financial Aid Director, 1700 South Main, Goshen, IN 46526, (219) 535-7525.

[240] GRACE THEOLOGICAL SEMINARY

ELIGIBILITY: Minority Academic Honor. Minority applicants who have achieved a 3.0 GPA or above in their baccalaureate studies and who present above-average GRE scores may qualify for a 50% tuition scholarship. These grants are renewable for succeeding semesters if a cumulative 3.0 GPA or above is maintained.
AMOUNT: Varies
CONTACT: Financial Aid Director, Grace Theological Seminary, 200 Seminary Drive, Winona Lake, IN 46590, (219) 267-8191.

[241] HALLIE Q. BROWN SCHOLARSHIP FUND

ELIGIBILITY: Minority students who are U.S. citizens with financial need and have applied to an accredited college or university.
AMOUNT: Up to $1,000
CONTACT: National Association of Colored Women's Clubs, 5808 16th Street, NW, Washington, DC 20011, (202) 726-2044.

[242] HARDIN-SIMMONS UNIVERSITY

ELIGIBILITY: The Texas National Baptist Scholarship Program. Must be recommended by the applicant's pastor. Must have graduated from a Texas High School, have a 2.0 GPA and be a black Baptist.
AMOUNT: $600

CONTACT: Financial Aid Office, Hardin-Simmons University, Drawer R/HSU Station, Abilene, TX 79698, (915) 670-1331.

[243] HAVERFORD COLLEGE
ELIGIBILITY: Class of 1912 Scholarship Fund assists students with financial need. When able, preference given to African or Asian students.
AMOUNT: Varies
CONTACT: Office of Admissions, Haverford College, Haverford, PA 19041-1392, (215) 896-1350.

[244] HAVERFORD COLLEGE
ELIGIBILITY: J. Henry Scattergood Scholarship Fund—to provide financial aid and other supportive services to black students.
AMOUNT: Varies
CONTACT: Office of Admissions, Haverford College, Haverford, PA 19041-1392, (215) 896-1350.

[245] HAVERFORD COLLEGE
ELIGIBILITY: Ira De A. Reid Scholarships for black and Hispanic students based on academic and personal promise. Dr. Reid was chairman of Haverford's sociology and anthropology department until retiring in 1966. His research centered on the conditions of blacks here and in the Caribbean, and his works include *In a Minor Key* and *The Negro Immigrant*. The amount of aid depends upon financial need. All awards are in the forms of grants and do not include loans or jobs. Deadline for admission and Financial Aid Form is January 31. Application fee can be waived. A campus interview is preferred.
AMOUNT: Varies
CONTACT: Director of Admissions, Haverford College, Haverford, PA 19041-1392, (215) 896-1350.

[246] HEALTH CAREERS OPPORTUNITY PROGRAM GRANTS

ELIGIBILITY: Assistance provided for education in health professions and students with financial need. Deadline November.
AMOUNT: Varies
CONTACT: Health Resources and Services Administration, Attn: Bureau of Health Professions, Division of Disadvantaged Assistance, Parklawn Building, Room 8A-09, 5600 Fishers Lane, Rockville, MD 20857, (301) 443-4493, Fax: (301) 443-5242.

[247] HERBERT LEHMAN EDUCATION FUND

ELIGIBILITY: Awarded to a black senior who is planning to attend desegregated and publicly supported colleges or universities in the South, who is a U.S. citizen, and who can show financial need. Deadline April 15.
AMOUNT: $1,200
CONTACT: Herbert Lehman Education Fund, Inc., Attn: NAACP Legal Defense, 99 Hudson Street, Suite 1600, New York, NY 10013, (212) 219-1900.

[248] HOLY CROSS COLLEGE

ELIGIBILITY: Martin Luther King, Jr. Scholarship offered to minority students until graduation. The student has a choice of making up the difference in tuition after the scholarship with either work-study or loans.
AMOUNT: Varies
CONTACT: Holy Cross College, c/o Financial Aid Office, One College Hill, Worcester, MA 01610, (508) 793-2443.

[249] UNIVERSITY OF HOUSTON

ELIGIBILITY: AICPA Scholarship is available to full-time minority students pursuing an accounting or taxation degree. Selection based on demonstrated financial need and satisfactory academic progress. Must have a 2.0 GPA. Deadline March 1.
AMOUNT: Varies
CONTACT: College of Business Administration, University of Hous-

ton, University Park, 4800 Calhoun, 106 H, Houston, TX 77004, (713) 749-2911.

---

[250] UNIVERSITY OF HOUSTON
ELIGIBILITY: Ethnic Recruitment Scholarships are awarded to entering freshmen who are minority residents of Texas with demonstrated financial need. Applicants must have a minimum SAT combined score of 900 or a minimum ACT composite score of 20. Financial need required. Deadline is March 1.
CONTACT: Financial Aid Director, University of Houston, University Park, Houston, TX 77004, (713) 749-3311.

---

[251] UNIVERSITY OF HOUSTON
ELIGIBILITY: The Shell Incentive Scholarship is awarded to entering minority students on the basis of demonstrated financial need. Must be a U.S. citizen. Deadline March 1.
AMOUNT: Varies
CONTACT: Cullen College of Engineering, University of Houston, University Park, 4800 Calhoun, 202 D, Houston, TX 77004, (713) 749-2401.

---

[252] UNIVERSITY OF HOUSTON
ELIGIBILITY: The Carnation Incentive Award is awarded to full-time minority education majors on the basis of demonstrated academic progress. Must have a minimum 3.0 GPA. Deadline March 1.
AMOUNT: Varies
CONTACT: College of Education, University of Houston, University Park, 4800 Calhoun, 214 FH, Houston, TX 77004, (713) 749-7407.

---

[253] UNIVERSITY OF HOUSTON
ELIGIBILITY: The Dow Chemical Company Scholarship is available to full-time minority students who are majoring in chemistry. Applicants must be U.S. citizens and demonstrate satisfactory academic progress. Deadline March 1.

AMOUNT: Varies
CONTACT: Natural Science/Math Department, University of Houston, University Park, 4800 Calhoun, 214 SR, Houston, TX 77004, (713) 749-4612.

[254] UNIVERSITY OF HOUSTON
ELIGIBILITY: The Amoco Foundation Scholarship is awarded to full-time, first-year minority students majoring in geology or geophysics who show satisfactory academic progress. Deadline March 1.
AMOUNT: Varies
CONTACT: Geosciences Dept., University of Houston, University Park, 4800 Calhoun, 214 SR Houston, TX 77004, (713) 749-3868.

[255] COLLEGE OF IDAHO, ASSOCIATION OF AFFIRMATIVE ACTION SCHOLARSHIP
ELIGIBILITY: Awarded annually to a minority student.
AMOUNT: $1,500
CONTACT: Financial Aid Director, The College of Idaho, 2112 Cleveland Blvd., Caldwell, ID 83605-9990, (208) 459-5308.

[256] INDIANA UNIVERSITY
ELIGIBILITY: Minority Achievers Program. Awards for entering or transferring minority students who demonstrate superior talent and high academic potential. Deadline March 1.
AMOUNT: $2,000 - $7,000
CONTACT: Dr. Herman Hudson, MAP Scholarships, M20 Memorial Hall, Indiana University, Bloomington, IN 47405, (812) 855-7853.

[257] INDIANA UNIVERSITY
ELIGIBILITY: Howard Jones Scholarship Fund. Awards to minority students in business administration or management with a minimum 3.3 GPA and financial need.
AMOUNT: $1,000
CONTACT: Indiana University, Attn: School of Business, Business

230, Bloomington, IN 47405, (812) 855-8066.

---

[258] INDIANA UNIVERSITY CENTER ON PHILANTHROPY

ELIGIBILITY: Doctoral Fellowships in the Study of Philanthropy. Research Grants in the Study of Philanthropy. Deadline February 15.
AMOUNT: Varies
CONTACT: Indiana University Center on Philanthropy, Research Office, 550 West North Street, Suite 301, Indianapolis, IN 46202-3162, (317) 274-8490.

---

[259] INROADS/NASHVILLE INC. INTERNSHIPS

ELIGIBILITY: The internships take place during the summer with a possibility of future full-time employment. Black students in their freshman or sophomore year, with a 3.3 GPA and majoring in business administration/management or engineering are eligible.
CONTACT: Inroads/Nashville, Inc., P.O. Box 3111, Nashville, TN 37219, (615) 255-7397.

---

[260] INSTITUTE FOR REAL ESTATE MANAGEMENT FOUNDATION GEORGE M. BROOKER COLLEGIATE SCHOLARSHIP FOR MINORITIES

ELIGIBILITY: Graduate and undergraduate minority students entering careers in real estate and specifically real estate management. Applicants must have declared a major in real estate or related field; must have completed two courses in real estate; must have at least a 3.0 GPA within major; must have recommendation letters, themed essay, and official transcripts. Deadline March 15.
AMOUNT: $1,000 for undergraduates, $2,500 for graduate students
CONTACT: Institute for Real Estate Managment Foundation, Attn: Foundation Coordinator, 430 North Michigan Avenue, P.O. Box 109025, Chicago, IL 60611-4090, (312) 329-6008.

---

[261] IOTA PHI LAMBDA BUSINESS SORORITY

ELIGIBILITY: Scholarships are offered to minority female under-graduates interested in business careers.
AMOUNT: Varies
CONTACT: Iota Phi Lambda Business Sorority, 811 E. 116 Street, Los Angeles, CA 90059.

---

[262] IOTA PHI LAMBDA SCHOLARSHIP PROGRAM

ELIGIBILITY: Award to increase interest in business among black women.
AMOUNT: Varies
CONTACT: Iota Phi Lambda Scholarship Program, 1062 West Pearl, Jackson, MS 39203.

---

[263] IOTA PHI LAMBDA SCHOLARSHIP PROGRAM

ELIGIBILITY: Black female high school students interested in business education.
AMOUNT: Varies
CONTACT: Iota Phi Lambda Sorority, Inc., c/o Dr. Evelyn Peevy, 5313 Halter Lane, Norfolk, VA 23502.

---

[264] IOWA STATE UNIVERSITY

ELIGIBILITY: Agricultural Career Awareness Scholarship Must be a minority student majoring in agriculture with a 2.0 GPA. Deadline January 1.
AMOUNT: $1,000
CONTACT: Extension Service Agent, Iowa State University, 32 Curtiss Hall, State 4-H Office, Ames, IA 50011, (515) 294-1017.

---

[265] IOWA STATE UNIVERSITY

ELIGIBILITY: Freshman Engineering Scholarships. Applicant must be a minority. Scholarship application available from student financial aid office. Deadline is December 1.
AMOUNT: $500

CONTACT: Scholarship Coordinator, Iowa State University, 101 Marston Hall, College of Engineering, Ames, IA 50011, (515) 294-1019.

[266] UNIVERSITY OF IOWA
ELIGIBILITY: Minority Engineering Education Effort Awards are available to minority students majoring in one of the following engineering areas: chemical, electrical, mechanical, civil or industrial. Financial need required.
AMOUNT: $250 to $2,500
CONTACT: Financial Aid Director, University of Iowa, Iowa City, IA 52242, (319) 353-2121.

[267] UNIVERSITY OF IOWA
ELIGIBILITY: Opportunity at Iowa Scholarship Program. Applicants must be U.S. minority students. Deadline December 8.
AMOUNT: Full tuition
CONTACT: Scholarship Chairman, University of Iowa, Office of Financial Aid, Iowa City, IA 52242, (800) 272-6412.

[268] THE IVIES
ELIGIBILITY: The Ivies helps minority students obtain financial aid and gain admission to Ivy League universities: Dartmouth, Penn, Princeton, Cornell, MIT, Brown, Yale, Columbia, and Harvard-Radcliffe.
AMOUNT: Varies
CONTACT: The Ivies, P.O. Box 1502A, Yale Station, New Haven, CT 06502.

[269] THE JACKIE ROBINSON EDUCATION AND LEADERSHIP DEVELOPMENT PROGRAM
ELIGIBILITY: Must show academic performance, leadership potential, financial need and commitment to the community. Deadline April 15.
AMOUNT: Up to $20,000 for four years.
CONTACT: The Jackie Robinson Scholarship, The Jackie Robinson Foundation, 3 West 35th Street, New York, NY 10001-2204, (212) 290-8600

[270] JACKIE ROBINSON FOUNDATION SCHOLARSHIP FUND

ELIGIBILITY: Minority students who are high school seniors, have demonstrated high academic achievements, financial need, leadership potential, and have been accepted to an accredited four-year institution. Deadline April 1.
AMOUNT: Varies
CONTACT: The Jackie Robinson Scholarship, The Jackie Robinson Foundation, 3 West 35th Street, New York, NY 10001-2204, (212) 290-8600

---

[271] JACKSON STATE UNIVERSITY

ELIGIBILITY: Hearin-Hess Scholarship Fund for computer science majors.
AMOUNT: $5,000
CONTACT: Dr. Maria Luisa Alvarez Harvey, Dean, W.E.B. DuBois Honors College, Jackson State University, Jackson, MS 39217, (601) 968-2107.

---

[272] JAMES ARCHITECTS & ENGINEERS MINORITY SCHOLARSHIP FOR THE STUDY OF ARCHITECTURE

ELIGIBILITY: To be eligible for the scholarship, the student must be black, be a high school senior in Indiana, rank in the upper one-quarter of the graduating class (or be recommended by the principal), have been accepted to study architecture or architectural engineering at an accredited institution, and demonstrate financial need. Deadline February.
AMOUNT: $1,000 up to five years
CONTACT: James Architects & Engineers, Inc., 120 Monument Circle, Suite 122, Indianapolis, IN 46204, (317) 631-0880.

---

[273] JEAN FLINT SCHOLARSHIP

ELIGIBILITY: This scholarship is to benefit the graduates of the Springfield, Massachusetts, public school system. Awarded to academically promising students of color who demonstrate financial need.

AMOUNT: Two awards of $3,000 to $5,000
CONTACT: Hampshire College, Attn: Financial Aid Director, Amherst, MA 01002, (413) 582-5484.

---

[274] JOHNSON & JOHNSON LEADERSHIP AWARDS PROGRAM

ELIGIBILITY: This program is available to minority men and women holding an undergraduate degree in any discipline for graduate study towards an MBA degree at one of seven selected institutions. Selection is based upon exceptional leadership ability and a strong interest in corporate management. Deadline January 31.
AMOUNT: $30,000
CONTACT: Johnson & Johnson Awards, United Negro College Fund, 500 East 62nd Street, New York, NY 10021, (212) 326-1239.

---

[275] JOSEPH EHRENREICH/NATIONAL PRESS PHOTOGRAPHERS ASSOCIATION SCHOLARSHIP

ELIGIBILITY: Students enrolled in a recognized 4-year college or university studying photojournalism. Financial need required.
AMOUNT: $1,000
CONTACT: National Press Photographers Association, P.O. Box 1146, Durham, NC 27702, (919) 489-3700.

---

[276] KANSAS NEWMAN COLLEGE MINORITY GRANT

ELIGIBILITY: Granted to minority student with 2.25 GPA who has been active in high school, church, and/or community. Letter of reference and special application required. Deadline August 1.
AMOUNT: up to $1,000
CONTACT: Kansas Newman College, Attn: Director of Financial Aid, 3100 McCormick Avenue, Wichita, KS 67213-2097, (316) 942-4291.

---

[277] KANSAS STATE UNIVERSITY

ELIGIBILITY: Academic Achievement and Leadership scholarships for undergraduate minority students who are Asian-American, African-

American, Hispanic American, Mexican American or Native American. Applicants must demonstrate outstanding academic and leadership accomplishments. First-year, transfer or returning students are eligible for awards. Applicants must submit a description of activities and goals and have a 3.0 GPA. Deadline is February 1.
AMOUNT: $400 to $1,000
CONTACT: Academic Achievement & Leadership Awards Committee, Office of Admissions, Anderson Hall, Kansas State University, Manhattan, KS 66505, (913) 532-6250 in Kansas, (800) 432-8270 outside.

[278] KANSAS STATE UNIVERSITY
ELIGIBILITY: Minority Engineering Education Effort. Financial need required and must be majoring in one of the following engineering areas: chemical, electrical, mechanical, civil, industrial, nuclear or agricultural.
AMOUNT: $250 to $2,500
CONTACT: Kansas State University, Dept. of Engineering, Manhattan, KS 66502, (212) 867-1100.

[279] UNIVERSITY OF KANSAS
ELIGIBILITY: Minority Scholarships, Nursing.
AMOUNT: Varies
CONTACT: Dean, School of Nursing, University of Kansas Medical School, Kansas City, KS 66045, (913) 588-1600.

[280] UNIVERSITY OF KANSAS
ELIGIBILITY: Scholarships are available for minorities majoring in journalism.
AMOUNT: Varies
CONTACT: Dean, School of Students, University of Kansas, 200 Stauffer Flint School of Journalism, Lawrence, KS 66045, (913) 864-4755.

[281] UNIVERSITY OF KANSAS
ELIGIBILITY: Minority Scholarship, Pharmacy.
AMOUNT: Varies
CONTACT: Dean of School of Pharmacy, University of Kansas, 2056 Malott School of Pharmacy, Lawrence, KS 66045, (913) 864-3591.

[282] UNIVERSITY OF KANSAS
ELIGIBILITY: Minority Scholarships.
AMOUNT: Varies
CONTACT: Office of the Dean, University of Kansas, College of Liberal Arts and Science, Lawrence, KS 66045, (913) 864-3661.

[283] KAPPA ALPHA PSI FRATERNITY
ELIGIBILITY: The fraternity's national service program "Guide Right" mandates each of its approximately 520 chapters to administer scholarships.
AMOUNT: Varies
CONTACT: Kappa Alpha Psi Fraternity, Inc., 2320 No. Broad Street, Philadelphia, PA 19132, (215) 228-7184.

[284] KELLOGG LEADERSHIP GRANT
ELIGIBILITY: Grant is for graduates of the minority fellowship programs seeking post-doctoral training in the form of leadership seminars and internships. Deadline January 15.
CONTACT: American Nurses Association Minority Fellowship Programs, 600 Maryland Avenue, SW, Suite 100W, Washington, DC 20024-2571, (202) 651-7246.

[285] KEN INOUYE MEMORIAL SCHOLARSHIP
ELIGIBILITY: Those eligible to apply must be currently enrolled in Los Angeles chapter schools. Selection is based on proven ability in journalism, potential, and financial need. Deadline March.
AMOUNT: $1,000
CONTACT: Society of Professional Journalists/L.A., C/O Greater Los

Angeles Press Club, 600 N. Vermont, Los Angeles, CA 90004, (213) 469-8180.

[286] KENDALL COLLEGE OF ART & DESIGN
ELIGIBILITY: Scholarships are awarded to black U.S. citizens with a 2.7 GPA. Renewable providing recipient meets established criteria and funds are available. Deadline March 15.
AMOUNT: $800
CONTACT: Kendall College of Art and Design, 111 Division Avenue, North Grand Rapids, MI 49503, (616) 451-2787.

[287] KENT STATE UNIVERSITY
ELIGIBILITY: Gives Oscar Ritchie Memorial Scholarships to academically talented black, Hispanic and Native American high school juniors. Awards of full tuition plus room and board costs are made based on an examination. Applicants must have a 3.25 GPA, show leadership qualities and participate in extracurricular activities. In 1947, Oscar Ritchie was the first black appointed to a faculty position at any state university in Ohio when he joined Kent State's sociology department.
CONTACT: Linda Lanier, Assistant Director of Admissions, Kent State University, Kent, OH 44242-0001, (216) 672-2444.

[288] UNIVERSITY OF KENTUCKY
ELIGIBILITY: Awards include the Journalism Award and the King Scholarship Fund, open to black residents of Kentucky.
AMOUNT: Varies
CONTACT: Office of Admissions, University of Kentucky, Lexington, KY 40506, (606) 257-7148.

[289] KNTV MINORITY SCHOLARSHIP
ELIGIBILITY: Awarded to a full-time student majoring in radio/TV broadcasting at a four-year California institution. Must show interest in television, need, involvement in the community, academics, and career aspirations. Deadline April 14.

AMOUNT: $1,000
CONTACT: KNTV Channel 11, Attn: Scholarship Board, 645 Park Avenue, San Jose, CA 9110, (408) 286-1111.

---

[290] KODAK MINORITY ACADEMIC AWARDS

ELIGIBILITY: Awards granted at 27 selected colleges to minority freshman majoring in one of the following: engineering, computer science/data processing, business administration/management, chemistry or accounting.
AMOUNT: 50% tuition
CONTACT: Scholarship Officer, Eastman Kodak Company, 343 State Street, Rochester, NY 14650, (716) 724-3127.

---

[291] KODAK SCHOLARSHIP AND INTERNSHIP PROGRAM

ELIGIBILITY: Available to students pursuing degrees in engineering, chemistry, polymer science, quantitative business analysis, computer science, marketing, finance, and accounting. Applicants must demonstrate academic excellence and personal leadership.
AMOUNT: Varies
CONTACT: Robert M. Belmont, Coordinator, Internship and Scholarship Program, Eastman Kodak Company, Personnel Resources, 343 State Street, Rochester, NY 14650, (716) 724-7593.

---

[292] KOPPERS INDUSTRY

ELIGIBILITY: Grants for minority and female engineering students in chemical, mechanical, or electrical engineering. Koppers awards funds to engineering departments and leaves the selection process to the college.
AMOUNT: Varies
CONTACT: Koppers Industry, 436 7th Avenue, Pittsburgh, PA 15219, (412) 227-2001.

---

[293] KRAFT, INC.-NATIONAL URBAN LEAGUE SCHOLARSHIP PROGRAM

ELIGIBILITY: Minority undergraduate students who are classified as juniors and who are pursuing full-time studies in engineering, sales, marketing, manufacturing operations, and finance and business administration are eligible. Students must be in the top 25 percent of their class.
AMOUNT: Varies
CONTACT: Northern Virginia Urban League, 901 N. Washington Street, Suite 202, Alexandria, VA 22314.

[294] LAKE ERIE COLLEGE MINORITY SCHOLARSHIP

ELIGIBILITY: Awarded to outstanding minority students with a 2.75 GPA who show promise of distinction in their field. Deadline March 1.
AMOUNT: $1,000
CONTACT: Lake Erie College, Attn: Director of Financial Aid, 391 W. Washington Street, Box 360, Painesville, OH 44077, (800) 533-4996.

[295] LA ROCHE COLLEGE, SISTERS OF THE DIVINE PROVIDENCE

ELIGIBILITY: Awarded to minority student with a 3.0 GPA. Must submit a typewritten essay describing activities participated in the past two years. Deadline May 1.
AMOUNT: $6,000
CONTACT: La Roche College, Attn: Financial Aid Director, 9000 Babcock Boulevard, Pittsburgh, PA 15237-5898, (412) 367-9300.

[296] LA SALLE UNIVERSITY

ELIGIBILITY: Community Academic Opportunity Grant. Awarded to minority students in the upper 1/5 of their graduating class. Contact high school counselor for application. Deadline February 15.
AMOUNT: up to Tuition
CONTACT: La Salle University, Attn: Academic Discovery Program, 20th Street and Olney Avenue, Philadelphia, PA 19141, (215) 951-1084.

[297] LAWRENCE TECHNOLOGICAL UNIVERSITY
ELIGIBILITY: Must be majoring in electrical or mechanical engineering. Financial need required. Deadline June 1.
AMOUNT: $250 to $2,500
CONTACT: Engineering Dept. Chairman, Lawrence Technological University, 21000 W. Ten Mile Road, Southfield, MI 48075, (313) 356-0200.

[298] LE MOYNE COLLEGE
ELIGIBILITY: Urban League Scholarship is awarded to an entering black freshman. Award will meet student's full need. No self-help is required in freshman year. Financial need required. Deadline February 15.
AMOUNT: Varies
CONTACT: Le Moyne College, Office of Financial Aid, Le Moyne Heights, Syracuse, NY 13214, (315) 445-4400.

[299] LEE ELDER SCHOLARSHIP FUND
ELIGIBILITY: The Lee Elder Scholarships are awarded to minorities who show financial need. Also taken into consideration are achievements and career goals.
AMOUNT: Varies
CONTACT: Lee Elder Scholarship Fund, 1725 K Street, NW, Suite 1201, Washington D.C. 20006.

[300] LINCOLN UNIVERSITY
ELIGIBILITY: The KTVI Scholarship is available to minority students or women who live within an 85 mile radius of St. Louis and are majoring in radio/TV or mass communications. Deadline April 1.
AMOUNT: Varies
CONTACT: Financial Aid Director, Lincoln University, 820 Chestnut, Jefferson City, MO 65101, (314) 681-5599.

[301] LONG ISLAND UNIVERSITY

ELIGIBILITY: Martin Luther King, Jr., Scholarships are available to black applicants who have financial need. Minimum combined SAT score of 900 and a 3.0 GPA is required. Deadline May 15.
AMOUNT: Varies
CONTACT: Director of Admissions, Long Island University, Brooklyn Center, University Plaza, Brooklyn, NY 11201-9926, (212) 834-6000.

[302] LORAS COLLEGE

ELIGIBILITY: Diversity Scholarships. Awarded to minority full-time students.
AMOUNT: $600 to $2,500
CONTACT: Loras College, Attn: Office of Financial Planning, 1450 Alta Vista Street, Dubuque, IA 52004-0178, (319) 588-7136.

[303] LORAS COLLEGE

ELIGIBILITY: Enrichment Award Selection is based upon participation in on-campus college activities. The award is renewable.
AMOUNT: $400 to $800
CONTACT: Financial Aid Director, Loras College, P.O. Box 178, 1450 Alta Vista Street, Dubuque, IA 52004-0178, (313) 588-7136.

[304] LOUISIANA STATE UNIVERSITY

ELIGIBILITY: New York Times Multicultural Scholarship awarded to a minority student majoring in journalism or mass communications with a 2.0 GPA, a combined 850 SAT score, and a minimum 20 ACT score. Deadline March 1.
AMOUNT: Varies
CONTACT: Louisiana State University, Manship School of Mass Communications, Attn: Scholarship Coordinator, Baton Rouge, LA 70803-7202, (504) 388-2336.

[305] LOYOLA COLLEGE CLAVER SCHOLARSHIPS
ELIGIBILITY: Awarded to minority students on the basis of academic achievement. Applicants must be U.S. citizens and graduate in the top 1/5 of their high school class. Deadline February 1.
AMOUNT: Varies
CONTACT: Loyola College, Attn: Director of Financial Aid, 4501 North Charles Street, Baltimore, MD 21210-2699, (410) 617-2576.

[306] LOYOLA MARYMOUNT UNIVERSITY
ELIGIBILITY: Minority Engineering Effort. Must be majoring in one of the following engineering areas: chemical, mechanical, or civil. Financial need required.
AMOUNT: $250 to $2,500
CONTACT: Financial Aid Director, Loyola Marymount University, Loyola Blvd at West 80th, Los Angeles, CA 90045, (213) 642-2753.

[307] LOYOLA UNIVERSITY NEW ORLEANS
ELIGIBILITY: Louis Twomey Scholarship is available to entering black freshmen from the New Orleans area who have a minimum SAT combined score of 770, a minimum ACT composite score of 17, and a 3.0 GPA. Applicants must submit a recommendation from a counselor. Deadline: February 1.
AMOUNT: $4,000
CONTACT: Loyola University, 6363 St. Charles Avenue, New Orleans, LA 70118, (504) 865-3240.

[308] LULAC NATIONAL SCHOLARSHIP FUND (LNSF)
ELIGIBILITY: Minority students accepted to a two or four-year U.S. institution. ACT test required. Applicants must be U.S. citizens or legal residents.
AMOUNT: $200 - $1,000
CONTACT: Laura Benso, National Scholarship Coordinator, LULAC National Scholarship Foundation, 400 First Street, NW, Suite 716, Washington, DC 20001, (202) 347-1652.

[309] LUTHERAN CHURCH WOMEN

ELIGIBILITY: Awards annual stipends to minority women who wish to pursue postsecondary education. Applicants must be members of the Lutheran Church of America.
AMOUNT: $1,000
CONTACT: Lutheran Church Women, 2900 Queen Lane, Philadelphia, PA 19144, (215) 848-3418.

[310] LUTHERAN CHURCH WOMEN KEMP SCHOLARSHIP

ELIGIBILITY: To those interested in continuing education through undergraduate, graduate, professional, or vocational study and are members of the Lutheran Church of America. They may be women in their teens who are going directly to college from high school. Deadline February.
AMOUNT: $1,500
CONTACT: Lutheran Church Women, 2900 Queen Lane, Philadelphia, PA 19144, (215) 848-3418.

[311] LYNCHBURG COLLEGE

ELIGIBILITY: The Black Leadership Grant is awarded to black students who have completed 16 years in school. Deadline: June 1.
AMOUNT: Up to $3,000
CONTACT: Director of Admissions, Lynchburg College, Admissions Office, Lynchburg, VA 24501, (804) 522-8300.

[312] MANSFIELD UNIVERSITY

ELIGIBILITY: The Martin Luther King, Jr., Scholarship is available to an incoming black college freshman. Deadline April 3
AMOUNT: $1,000
CONTACT: Mansfield University, Mansfield, PA 16933, (717) 662-4243.

[313] MARVIN C. ZANDERS SCHOLARSHIP

ELIGIBILITY: Awarded to a black, full-time student with a 2.5 GPA and a resident of Florida. Applicants must demonstrate strong academics, need, and submit essay and recommendations. Deadline May 1.
AMOUNT: $500
CONTACT: Marvin C. Zanders Scholarship, c/o Mrs. Betty Baker, P.O. Box 993, Apopka, FL 32703.

[314] MARY BALDWIN COLLEGE

ELIGIBILITY: Baldwin Scholarships awarded to minority female students with a 3.0 GPA in the upper 1/5 of their class. Deadline March 1.
AMOUNT: $2,000 to $6,000
CONTACT: Mary Baldwin College, Attn: Director of Admissions, Staunton, VA 24401-9983, (703) 887-7022.

[315] MARYCREST COLLEGE

ELIGIBILITY: Honors Award/Minority Student Achievement. Granted to minorities who are U.S. citizens and show outstanding academic or personal achievement. Students must apply for admission to Marycrest and submit the Honors Award application form along with H.S. transcripts, ACT/SAT scores and letters of recommendation. Awards are renewable based on academic performance. Deadline March 15.
AMOUNT: $2,000 annually
CONTACT: Financial Aid Director, Marycrest College, 1607 West 12th Street, Davenport, IA 52804, (319) 326-9512.

[316] MARYLAND STATE BOARD OF HIGHER EDUCATION

ELIGIBILITY: Graduate/Professional Programs. The program is intended to encourage the enrollment of students from races other than the predominant one on the student's campus. Applicants must be residents of Maryland. State public colleges administer this program.
AMOUNT: $500
CONTACT: State Board of Higher Education, The Jeffrey Bldg., 16 Francis Street, Suite 219, Annapolis, MD 21401, (301) 974-5370.

[317] UNIVERSITY OF MARYLAND

ELIGIBILITY: The Alpha Wives—Montgomery County Scholarship is awarded to a black woman with a 2.8 GPA. Must show financial need and be a single parent. Deadline March 6.

AMOUNT: $500

CONTACT: Office of Human Relations, University of Maryland, Black Women's Council, Room 1107, Hornbake Library, College Park, MD 20742, (301) 454-4124.

[318] UNIVERSITY OF MARYLAND

ELIGIBILITY: Applicants must be black, Hispanic, or American Indian and be U.S. citizens or permanent residents enrolled in a full-time undergraduate engineering program. Must have at least a 2.5 GPA. Deadline: May 1.

AMOUNT: $500 to $1,500

CONTACT: Director, Center for Minorities in Science and Engineering, University of Maryland, College Park, MD 20742, (301) 405-3880.

[319] UNIVERSITY OF MARYLAND

ELIGIBILITY: NUS Corporation Scholarship is awarded to black undergraduate students majoring in engineering. Must have a 3.0 GPA.

AMOUNT: Varies

CONTACT: University of Maryland, College of Engineering, College Park, MD 20742, (301) 454-0100.

[320] UNIVERSITY OF MARYLAND

ELIGIBILITY: The Benjamin Banneker Scholarship is available to entering black freshman students based on academic achievement. The award pays in-state tuition and fees for four years provided the recipient maintains a minimum 2.5 GPA and 12 credits/semester.

AMOUNT: In-state tuition

CONTACT: University of Maryland, North Administration Building, Room 0102B, College Park, MD 20742, (301) 454-4008.

[321] UNIVERSITY OF MARYLAND
ELIGIBILITY: George Phillips Scholarship Fund. Awarded to a full-time minority student with a 3.0 GPA who demonstrates financial need. Deadline May 1.
AMOUNT: Varies
CONTACT: University of Maryland, Attn: Scholarship Coordinator, 0102 Lee Building, College Park, MD 20742, (301) 314-8313.

[322] UNIVERSITY OF MARYLAND
ELIGIBILITY: Westinghouse Ramsey Scholarship. This renewable award is available to a minority student majoring in engineering or computer science.
AMOUNT: $1,500
CONTACT: Asst. Dean of Engineering, University of Maryland, Engineering Classroom Bldg., Room 1131L , College Park, MD 20742, (301) 454-4048.

[323] UNIVERSITY OF MARYLAND
ELIGIBILITY: The Volkswagen of America Scholarship is available to minority students majoring in computer science. Deadline March 1.
AMOUNT: $1,200
CONTACT: University of Maryland, Office of the Provost, College Park, MD 20742, (301) 454-0100.

[324] UNIVERSITY OF MARYLAND
ELIGIBILITY: ALCOA Engineering Scholarship is available to minority students enrolled in engineering programs. Deadline March 31.
AMOUNT: $250
CONTACT: University of Maryland, Center for Minority in Science and Engineering, College Park, MD 20742, (301) 454-0100.

[325] UNIVERSITY OF MARYLAND, BALTIMORE
ELIGIBILITY: Graduate Minority Fellowship. This fellowship can be renewed for one additional year. Applicants are selected for the award

based on professional and academic achievements in addition to recommendations from the faculty of University of Maryland, Baltimore.
AMOUNT: $10,000
CONTACT: University of Maryland, 5401 Wilkins Avenue, Baltimore, MD 21228, (410) 455-1000.

[326] UNIVERSITY OF MARYLAND, BALTIMORE
ELIGIBILITY: Meyerhoff Scholarship awarded to black student with a 3.0 GPA majoring in architecture or engineering.
AMOUNT: Tuition and fees
CONTACT: University of Maryland, Baltimore County, Attn: Office of the President, 5401 Wilkens Avenue, Baltimore, MD 21228-5398, (410) 455-2291.

[327] UNIVERSITY OF MARYLAND, BALTIMORE
ELIGIBILITY: Scholastic Achievement Award. Awarded to minority student with a 3.0 GPA. Deadline March 1.
AMOUNT: $2,500
CONTACT: University of Maryland, Attn: Director of Financial Aid, Baltimore County, 5401 Wilkins Avenue, Baltimore, MD 21228, (410) 455-2387.

[328] MARYVILLE COLLEGE
ELIGIBILITY: Ethnic Minority Scholarship awarded to incoming freshmen demonstrating good academic promise and personal achievement. Must have a 2.5 GPA.
AMOUNT: Varies
CONTACT: Maryville College, Attn: Office of Financial Aid, 502 E. Lamar Alexander Highway, Maryville, TN 37801, (615) 981-8100.

[329] MARY WASHINGTON COLLEGE
ELIGIBILITY: Student must be a black U.S. citizen attending Mary Washington.
AMOUNT: Varies

CONTACT: Financial Aid Director, Mary Washington College, Fredericksburg, VA 22401-5358, (703) 899-4684.

---

[330] MAXWELL HOUSE COFFEE MINORITY SCHOLARSHIP
ELIGIBILITY: Applicants must be minority high school students or graduates from New York, Philadelphia, Detroit, Chicago, St. Louis, Baltimore, or Newark. Applicants must be willing to attend one of the black colleges participating in their local black college fairs.
AMOUNT: $3,000
CONTACT: Maxwell House Coffee, 250 North Street, White Plains, NY 10625, (914) 335-2500.

---

[331] MCKENDREE COLLEGE
ELIGIBILITY: Capital Cities Scholarship is available to qualified minority students.
AMOUNT: Varies
CONTACT: Financial Aid Director, McKendree College, 701 College Road, Lebanon, IL 62254, (618) 537-4481.

---

[332] MCKENDREE COLLEGE
ELIGIBILITY: The Eddie Hall Scholarship is available to academically qualified minority students. Must have a 3.0 GPA.
AMOUNT: Varies
CONTACT: Financial Aid Director, McKendree College, Lebanon, IL 62254, (618) 537-4481.

---

[333] THE MCKNIGHT DOCTORAL FELLOWSHIP PROGRAM
ELIGIBILITY: Fellowships are awarded in all disciplines except law, medicine, and education, with the exceptions of mathematics and science education and educational testing and measurement. Two fellowships are available in art history, art education, arts management, history, or literature to study the Barnett-Aden African American Art Collection

at the Museum of African American Art in Tampa, Florida. Deadline January 15.
AMOUNT: $16,000
CONTACT: The Florida Education Fund, 201 East Kennedy Boulevard, Suite 1525, Tampa, FL 33602, (813) 272-2772.

[334] MEDICAL LIBRARY ASSOCIATION
ELIGIBILITY: Minority Scholarship. Applicants must be members of a minority group and be entering an ALA accredited graduate library school or have at least one half of his/her academic requirements to complete during the first year following the granting of the scholarship. Deadline February 1.
AMOUNT: $2,000
CONTACT: Medical Library Association, 919 N. Michigan Avenue, Suite 3208, Chicago, IL 60611, (312) 266-2456.

[335] MEMPHIS STATE UNIVERSITY
ELIGIBILITY: Minority Scholarships. Must maintain a 2.8 GPA and 30 hour per semester service requirement. Deadline March 1.
AMOUNT: Registration fees/books
CONTACT: Scholarship Office/Student Aid, Memphis State University, Scates Hall, Memphis, TN 38152, (901) 678-2303.

[336] MEMPHIS STATE UNIVERSITY
ELIGIBILITY: Non-resident Minority Scholarship. Must maintain a 3.2 GPA and 30 hour per semester service requirement. Deadline is March 1.
AMOUNT: Varies
CONTACT: Scholarship Office/Student Aid, Memphis State University, Scates Hall, Memphis, TN 38152, (901) 678-2303.

[337] MERCER COUNTY COMMUNITY COLLEGE

ELIGIBILITY: The Forum for Minority Concerns Award is awarded to black students for academic excellence, community service and special achievements.

CONTACT: Mercer County Community College, P.O. Box 8, Trenton, NJ 08690, (609) 586-4800.

[338] MERCER COUNTY COMMUNITY COLLEGE

ELIGIBILITY: Dental Assisting Conference Award. Two annual awards to dental assisting certificate students with the highest GPAs completing the first semester of the program. At least one award is reserved for a minority student.

CONTACT: Financial Aid Director, Mercer County Community College, P.O. Box 8, Trenton, NJ 08690, (609) 586-4800.

[339] MERCYHURST COLLEGE

ELIGIBILITY: Bishop Meyers Scholarship. Awarded to minority student in the top 1/5 of their high school class with a minimum combined 800 SAT score. Deadline March 15.

AMOUNT: $2,500 to $5,000

CONTACT: Mercyhurst College, Attn: Director of Admissions, Glenwood Hills, Erie, PA 16546, (814) 825-0200.

[340] MERCYHURST COLLEGE

ELIGIBILITY: Dr. Charles Richard Drew Scholarships are available for black students with a 2.5 GPA and in the top half of their class.

AMOUNT: $2,000

CONTACT: Director of Admissions, Mercyhurst College, Glenwood Hills, Erie, PA 16546, (814) 825-0200.

[341] MERRIMACK COLLEGE

ELIGIBILITY: Technical Training Foundation Scholarships. These scholarships are renewable provided that the recipient maintains satisfactory academic progress. Must be majoring or plan to major in computer

science or electrical engineering.
AMOUNT: Varies
CONTACT: Director of Financial Aid, Merrimack College, Office of Financial Aid, North Andover, MA 01845, (617) 683-7111.

[342] MESSIAH COLLEGE
ELIGIBILITY: Minority Student Grants are available to full-time, non-caucasian U.S. citizens, with priority given to students with the greatest demonstrated financial need.
AMOUNT: $3,000
CONTACT: Financial Aid Director, Messiah College, Grantham, PA 17027, (717) 766-2511.

[343] MIAMI UNIVERSITY, OHIO
ELIGIBILITY: FAF and FA application. 2/3 gift and 1/3 self-help.
AMOUNT: $200 to $7,600
CONTACT: Miami University, Ohio, Edwards House, Oxford, OH 45056, (513) 529-5757.

[344] MIAMI UNIVERSITY, OHIO
ELIGIBILITY: Black Scholars Program. Awarded to black student with a 2.5 GPA, combined 1000 SAT score or 20 ACT score. Deadline January 31.
AMOUNT: $1,600 to $3,000
CONTACT: Miami University, Ohio, Attn: Office of Financial Aid, Edwards House, Oxford, OH 45056, (513) 529-4734.

[345] MIAMI UNIVERSITY, OHIO
ELIGIBILITY: Black Student Achievement Grant. Applicant must have a 21 ACT score and demonstrate financial need. Deadline January 31.
AMOUNT: up to $2,000
CONTACT: Miami University, Ohio, Attn: Office of Financial Aid, Edwards House, Oxford, OH 45056, (513) 529-4734.

[346] MIAMI UNIVERSITY, OHIO

ELIGIBILITY: Minority Scholars Program. Awarded to a minority student other than black with a minimum 2.5 GPA, a combined 1000 SAT score or a 26 ACT score. Deadline January 31.
AMOUNT: $1,000
CONTACT: Miami University, Ohio, Attn: Office of Financial Aid, Edwards House, Oxford, OH 45056, (513) 529-4734.

[347] MICHIGAN STATE UNIVERSITY

ELIGIBILITY: Distinguished Minority Freshman. Awarded to a minority freshman in the upper 1/5 of their high school graduating class. Deadline January 1.
AMOUNT: $4,000 to $10,000
CONTACT: Michigan State University, Attn: Office of Financial Aid, 252 Student Services Building, East Lansing, MI 48824-1113, (517) 353-5940.

[348] UNIVERSITY OF MICHIGAN SCHOLARSHIP

ELIGIBILITY: Applicants must be U.S. citizens, major in engineering and have a 3.0 GPA. Deadline December 4.
AMOUNT: $1,000 - 4 years
CONTACT: Financial Aid Office, University of Michigan, College of Engineering, 2417 EECS Bldg., Ann Arbor, MI 48109-2116, (313) 763-5050.

[349] MILWAUKEE INSTITUTE OF ART AND DESIGN

ELIGIBILITY: Awarded to a full-time fine or applied arts or design major at M.I.A.D. through a portfolio competition. Deadline February 1.
AMOUNT: $3,500
CONTACT: Milwaukee Institute of Art and Design, Attn: Financial Aid Officer, 273 East Erie Street, Milwaukee, WI 53202, (414) 276-7889.

[350] MINORITY BIOMEDICAL RESEARCH SUPPORT (MBRS) PROGRAM

ELIGIBILITY: Program is aimed toward ensuring minority groups an equal opportunity to pursue careers in biomedical research. The program provides for academic year and summer salaries and wages for faculty, students, and support personnel needed to conduct a research project.
AMOUNT: Varies
CONTACT: Program Administrator, National Institutes of Health, Div. of Research Resources, Bldg. 31, Room 5B35, Bethesda, MD 20892, (301) 496-6745.

[351] MINORITY EDUCATION FUND

ELIGIBILITY: Minority students admitted to a college who are members of an RCA Church or enrolled in an RCA college.
AMOUNT: Varies
CONTACT: Reformed Church of America (RCA) , 475 Riverside Drive, Room 1819, New York, NY 10027, (212) 870-3071.

[352] MINORITY LEADERS FELLOWSHIP PROGRAM

ELIGIBILITY: The Washington Center's Minority Leaders Fellowship Program selects a group of outstanding college students to spend ten weeks in Washington, DC. Students explore the field of leadership not only as a theoretical concept but also as a daily reality. Applicants must be nominated by the president of their college or university.
AMOUNT: Varies
CONTACT: The Washington Public Affairs Center, 512 Tenth Street, NW, Suite 600, Washington, DC 20004, (202) 638-4949.

[353] MINORITY PRESENCE/NORTH CAROLINA DOCTORAL/LAW/VETERINARY MEDICINE PROGRAM

ELIGIBILITY: Black North Carolinians enrolled full time in a doctoral degree program at East Carolina University, North Carolina State University, the University of North Carolina at Chapel Hill, the University of North Carolina at Greensboro, the Law School at the University of North

Carolina at Chapel Hill, or in the School of Veterinary Medicine at North Carolina State University. Applications are available at each school.
AMOUNT: $4,000
CONTACT: North Carolina State Education Assistance Program, P.O. Box 2688, Chapel Hill, NC 27515-2688, (919) 549-8614.

[354] MINORITY SCHOLARSHIP PROGRAM
ELIGIBILITY: Synod of the Trinity. Applicants must submit a narrative of career goals and family situation, along with the application. Award eligibility includes residents of all counties of West Virginia except those in the panhandles (NE & SW counties). The applicant must register with his/her financial aid office and apply for federal (Pell) and state programs. A transcript of grades must also be filed.
AMOUNT: $200 to $800
CONTACT: Minority Scholarship Program, 3040 Market Street, Camp Hill, PA 17011-4591, (717) 737-0421.

[355] MINORITY TEACHER SCHOLARSHIP
ELIGIBILITY: Applicants must be U.S. citizens, attend an Indiana Institution full-time and major in education. Must teach 3 out of 5 years in Indiana.
AMOUNT: $1,000
CONTACT: Student Assistance Commission, 964 N. Pennsylvania Street, Indianapolis, IN 46204, (317) 232-2350.

[356] MISSISSIPPI STATE UNIVERSITY
ELIGIBILITY: Minority Engineering Effort. Financial need required. Must be majoring in agriculture or one of the following engineering areas: electrical, biomedical, civil, nuclear, aerospace, chemical, industrial, or petroleum.
AMOUNT: Varies
CONTACT: Institutional Research Office, Mississippi State University, Drawer EY, Mississippi State, MS 39762, (601) 325-3221.

[357] UNIVERSITY OF MISSISSIPPI
ELIGIBILITY: Minority Engineering Effort for those majoring in engineering. Financial need required. Deadline August 15.
AMOUNT: $250 to $2,500
CONTACT: Financial Aid Director, University of Mississippi, University, MS 38677, (601) 232-8411.

[358] UNIVERSITY OF MISSOURI
ELIGIBILITY: George Washington Carver Graduate Fellowship awards an assistantship stipend for a minority student who will work for the Missouri Agriculture Station. Must be a master of science/doctor of philosophy candidate. Must be majoring in one of the following: fisheries, wildlife resource/management, agriculture, animal science, chemistry-biology, horticulture, plant sciences, forestry, engineer-agriculture, agribusiness, atmospheric sciences, entomology, food science technology/nutrition or sociology.
AMOUNT: Varies
CONTACT: Dean, College of Agriculture, University of Missouri, Agriculture Bldg. 2-64, Columbia, MO 65211, (314) 882-2121.

[359] MONMOUTH COLLEGE
ELIGIBILITY: Margaret Doxey Memorial Scholarship. Awarded to a promising female student who demonstrates financial need. Deadline February 1.
AMOUNT: Varies
CONTACT: Monmouth College, Attn: Director of Admissions, Office of Admissions, West Long Branch, NJ 07764-1898, (908) 571-3456.

[360] MONTGOMERY COLLEGE
ELIGIBILITY: ORI, Incorporated Scholarship. Applicants must be full-time minority students who have completed a minimum of 24 credits with a 3.0 GPA. Must be a U.S. citizen majoring in one of the following areas: mathematics, physics, computer science/data processing or engineering. Financial need required. Deadline June 15.
AMOUNT: $1,140

CONTACT: Financial Aid Director, Montgomery College, Rockville, MD 20850, (301) 279-5000.

[361] MONTGOMERY COUNTY COMMUNITY COLLEGE

ELIGIBILITY: The Leonard Jones Memorial Scholarship is a book scholarship for a black freshman or sophomore in satisfactory standing. Financial need required. Deadline May 1.
AMOUNT: $50
CONTACT: Financial Aid Director, Montgomery County Community College, 340 DeKalb Pike, Blue Bell, PA 19422, (215) 641-6566.

[362] MOREHOUSE COLLEGE

ELIGIBILITY: The United Negro College Fund awards to black entering freshman. Must have a strong academic background. Apply early.
AMOUNT: $100 to $2,000
CONTACT: Morehouse College, 233 Chestnut Street, SW, Atlanta, GA 30314, (404) 681-2800.

[363] MOUNT MARY COLLEGE

ELIGIBILITY: The Tona Diebels Minority Scholarship is awarded to a minority freshman graduating in the upper 20% of their class with a 3.0 GPA. Applicants are to submit an essay demonstrating leadership qualities through involvement in a variety of extracurricular activities. The award is renewable. Female only. Deadline February 15.
AMOUNT: $500
CONTACT: Financial Aid Director, Mount Mary College, 2900 N. Menomonee River Pkwy., Milwaukee, WI 53222, (414) 259-9220.

[364] MOUNT ST. MARY'S COLLEGE

ELIGIBILITY: Funston V. Collins Grants are awarded to entering black students. These are renewable based on satisfactory progress. Although need is not a prerequisite, all recipients are required to file a FAF each year

and apply for any state or private assistance for which they may be eligible. Deadline January 1.
AMOUNT: $500 to $3,000
CONTACT: Financial Aid Director, Mount St. Mary's College, MD Financial Aid Office, Emmitsburg, MD 21727, (301) 447-5207.

---

[365] MOUNT UNION COLLEGE SCHOLARSHIPS
ELIGIBILITY: Scholarships are awarded to minority students in the upper 1/5 of their class. Must have a 3.0 GPA. Based on merit.
AMOUNT: $2,000
CONTACT: Office of Admissions, Mount Union College, 1972 Clark Avenue, Alliance, OH 44601, (216) 823-6050.

---

[366] MUNSON INSTITUTE OF AMERICAN MARITIME STUDIES
ELIGIBILITY: Paul Cuffe Memorial Fellowship for the Study of Minorities in American Maritime History. The fellowships are offered to encourage research that considers the participation of minorities in the maritime activities of New England. Applicants must send a full description of the proposed project, a preliminary bibliography, brief project budget, resume, and references. Deadline June 15.
AMOUNT: Up to $2,400
CONTACT: Director, Munson Institute of American Maritime Studies, Mystic Seaport Museum, P.O. Box 6000, Mystic, CT 06355-0990, (203) 572-5359, Fax: (203) 572-5329.

---

[367] MUSIC ASSISTANCE FUND SCHOLARSHIP PROGRAM
ELIGIBILITY: Minority students who need financial help to attend conservatories and schools of music, if they are interested in playing orchestral instruments.
AMOUNT: $250 to $1,000
CONTACT: The Music Assistance Fund, New York Philharmonic, Avery Fisher Hall, Broadway at 65th Street, New York, NY 10023, (212) 580-8700.

---

[368] MUSIC ASSISTANCE FUND

ELIGIBILITY: Applicants must intend to pursue a career in orchestral playing. Voice, piano, and conducting students not eligible. Audition is required. Deadline November 1.
AMOUNT: $500 to $2,000
CONTACT: Music Assistance Fund, Avery Fisher Hall, Lincoln Center, Broadway at 65th Street, New York, NY 10023, (212) 580-8700.

[369] MUSIC ASSISTANCE FUND

ELIGIBILITY: Financial aid to students who intend to pursue a professional career in symphony orchestra. Applicants must be a U.S. citizen. Deadline January 14.
AMOUNT: Up to $2,500
CONTACT: Music Assistance Fund, Attn: Awards Officer, American Symphony Orchestra League, 777 14th Street, NW, Suite 500, Washington, DC 20005-3201, (202) 628-0099.

[370] NAACP ACT-SO ACADEMIC, CULTURAL, TECHNOLOGICAL AND SCIENTIFIC OLYMPICS SCHOLARSHIPS

ELIGIBILITY: Scholarships are offered to black students who are winners in local NAACP competitions. Students also earn an expense-paid trip to the national competition usually held in June. Categories include the performing arts, humanities, visual arts and sciences. Deadline is usually 2 weeks before the national convention of ACT-SO.
AMOUNT: $500 to $1,000
CONTACT: Contact a local NAACP branch.

[371] NAACP AGNES JONES JACKSON SCHOLARSHIP

ELIGIBILITY: Awarded to full-time students under age 25 based on need, academic achievement, and NAACP involvement. High school seniors must have a 2.5 GPA. College undergraduates must have a 2.0 GPA. Deadline April 30.
AMOUNT: $1,500
CONTACT: NAACP, Attn: Education Department, 4805 Mount Hope Drive, Baltimore, MD 21215-3297, (410) 358-8900

[372] NAACP ROY WILKINS EDUCATION SCHOLARSHIP PROGRAM

ELIGIBILITY: Awarded to a black student with a 2.5 GPA, letters of recommendation, financial and grade transcripts, and need. Deadline April 30.
AMOUNT: $1,000
CONTACT: NAACP, Attn: Education Department, 4805 Mount Hope Drive, Baltimore, MD 21215-3297, (410) 358-8900.

[373] NAACP SCHOLARSHIP PROGRAM

ELIGIBILITY: Applicants must be members of the NAACP who are majoring in the fields of engineering, science, computer science, mathematics, or environmental science. Applicants must be U.S. citizens and be enrolled or accepted at an accredited college or university in the U.S. and are graduating high school seniors who rank in the top 1/3 of their class with a 3.0 GPA. Deadline April 30.
AMOUNT: Varies
CONTACT: Director of Education, NAACP, 4805 Mount Hope Drive, Baltimore, MD 21215, (410) 486-9135.

[374] NAACP SUTTON EDUCATION SCHOLARSHIP

ELIGIBILITY: Awarded to a black U.S. citizen with a 3.0 GPA. Applicant must be majoring in education. Must be active in the NAACP and show financial need. Deadline April 30.
AMOUNT: $1,000 to $2,000 renewable
CONTACT: Education Department, NAACP, 4805 Mt. Hope Drive, Baltimore, MD 21215-3297, (301) 358-8900.

[375] NAACP WILLEMS SCHOLARSHIP

ELIGIBILITY: The Willems Scholarship is awarded to a black U.S. citizen with a 3.0 GPA. Applicants must be majoring in mathematics, physics, engineering, or chemistry. Must be active in the NAACP.
AMOUNT: $2,000 to $3,000 renewable
CONTACT: Education Department, NAACP, 4805 Mt. Hope Road, Baltimore, MD 21215-3297, (301) 358-8900.

[376] NATIONAL ACHIEVEMENT SCHOLARSHIP PROGRAM FOR OUTSTANDING NEGRO STUDENTS

ELIGIBILITY: Black students who plan to earn a bachelor's degree. PSAT/NMSQT must be taken. Application, transcript, recommendations required.
AMOUNT: Varies.
CONTACT: NASP for Outstanding Negro Students, One Rotary Center, Evanston, IL 60201, (847) 866-05100.

[377] NATIONAL ACTION COUNCIL FOR MINORITIES IN ENGINEERING, INC.

ELIGIBILITY: Incentive Grant Program for needy minorities enrolled full-time in an undergraduate engineering program; also for entering freshmen and transfer students with at least 2.5 GPA.
AMOUNT: Varies
CONTACT: NACME, 3 West 35th Street, New York, NY 10001, (212) 279-2626.

[378] NATIONAL ASSOCIATION OF BLACK ACCOUNTANTS

ELIGIBILITY: The annual scholarship is awarded to a black student with a 3.5 GPA majoring in accounting. Recipient must attend annual convention, expenses paid. Deadline March 31.
AMOUNT: $2,500
CONTACT: Executive Director, National Assoc. Black Accountants, 300 I Street, NE, Suite 107, Washington, DC 20002, (202) 543-6656.

[379] NATIONAL ASSOCIATION OF BLACK JOURNALISTS

ELIGIBILITY: These scholarship program awards are for majors in journalism, photography, and radio/TV broadcasting enrolled in accredited four-year colleges. A 500-to-800 word article and three samples of work must be submitted. Apply late fall.
AMOUNT: $2,500

CONTACT: Executive Director, National Association of Black Journalists Scholarship Program, 11600 Sunrise Valley Drive, Reston, VA 22091, (703) 648-1283.

[380] NATIONAL ASSOCIATION OF BLACK WOMEN ATTORNEYS

ELIGIBILITY: Black women law students are eligible to enter this essay contest. The subject of the essay changes each year but always focuses on an issue of contemporary concern. Applicants must have completed 16 years in school.
AMOUNT: $1,000
CONTACT: National Association of Black Women Attorneys, 724 9th Street, NW, Suite 206, Washington, DC 20001, (202) 637-3570.

[381] NATIONAL ASSOCIATION OF MEDIA WOMEN, ATLANTA CHAPTER

ELIGIBILITY: Scholarship awarded to an undergraduate female minority student majoring in mass communications and attending an institution in Georgia.
AMOUNT: $5,000
CONTACT: National Association of Media Women—Atlanta Chapter, Attn: Chairperson, 1185 Niskey Lane Road, SW, Atlanta, GA 30331, (404) 344-5862.

[382] NATIONAL ASSOCIATION OF NEGRO MUSICIANS, INC.

ELIGIBILITY: Awards for minority students, ages 18 to 30, for instrumental and vocal music. Applicants must be sponsored by a local branch of the organization, must compete and win local, regional, and national competitions. Deadline July 1.
AMOUNT: $250 to $1,500
CONTACT: National Association of Negro Musicians, Inc., P.O. Box S-011, Chicago, IL 60628.

[383] NATIONAL BLACK CAUCUS OF LIBRARIANS

ELIGIBILITY: Charlemae Hill Rollins Scholarship is awarded to black college graduates who have an excellent academic record and have completed no more than 12 semester hours toward the graduate degree in librarianship if they are legal residents of the Chicago area. Recipients may attend any library school accredited by the American Library Association. Deadline March 1.

AMOUNT: $300

CONTACT: Chairman, Rollins Scholarship Comm., Chicago Chapter, National Black Caucus of Librarians, 6914 S. Morgan, Chicago, IL 60621, (312) 874-7534.

---

[384] NATIONAL BLACK MBA ASSOCIATION, INC.

ELIGIBILITY: MBA Scholarships for minority students enrolled in a full-time graduate or doctoral business program. Deadline March 31.

AMOUNT: $3,000 for master's, $5,000 to $10,000 for doctorate

CONTACT: MBA Scholarships, National Black MBA Association, Inc., 180 N. Michigan Avenue, Chicago, IL 60601, (312) 236-2622.

---

[385] NATIONAL BLACK NURSES' ASSOCIATION

ELIGIBILITY: Ambi-Nicholas Laboratories Scholarship. Awarded to black American nursing students belonging to a chapter of the National Black Nurses' Association and who are enrolled in a current program. Applicants must demonstrate academic excellence, professional commitment, personal integrity, active involvement in the black community, and financial need. Deadline May.

AMOUNT: Varies

CONTACT: National Black Nurses' Association, Inc., P.O. Box 18358, Boston, MA 02118, (617) 266-9703.

---

[386] NATIONAL BLACK NURSES' ASSOCIATION

ELIGIBILITY: Lauranne Sams Scholarship Award awarded to black nursing students who belong to a local chapter of the National Black Nurses' Association and who demonstrate academic excellence, professional commitment, personal integrity, and financial need. Deadline May.

AMOUNT: Varies
CONTACT: National Black Nurses' Assocation, Inc., P.O. Box 18358, Boston, MA 02118, (617) 266-9703.

---

[387] NATIONAL BLACK NURSES' ASSOCIATION

ELIGIBILITY: March of Dimes Birth Defect Award is given to a black nursing student with the best essay addressing the "Prevention of Teenage Pregnancy and Decrease in Infant Mortality Rates." Entrants must be members of the National Black Nurses' Assocation and must be enrolled in a LPN/LVN program, associate degree program, diploma program, or baccalaureate program. Essays are judged on the basis of the statement of the problem, proposal for dealing with the problem, clarity and innovation of the approach, grammar, style, clarity, and format (under 2500 words) . The competition is held annually and is co-sponsored by the March of Dimes Birth Defects Foundation. Deadline May.
AMOUNT: $1,000
CONTACT: National Black Nurses' Assocation, Inc., P.O. Box 18358, Boston, MA 02118, (617) 266-9703.

---

[388] NATIONAL BLACK POLICE ASSOCIATION

ELIGIBILITY: Must be a black U.S. citizen in the upper 3/5 of their class, have a 2.5 GPA, and majoring in law enforcement/police administration. Financial need required.
AMOUNT: $500
CONTACT: National Black Police Association, 1100 17th Street, NW, Suite 1000, Washington, DC 20036 , (202) 457-0563.

---

[389] NATIONAL CANCER INSTITUTE COMPREHENSIVE MINORITY BIOMEDICAL PROGRAM

ELIGIBILITY: This program is for minority scientists developing careers in cancer research.
AMOUNT: Varies
CONTACT: CMBP Program Director, National Cancer Institute, Div.

of Examural Activities, Building 31, Room 10A04, Bethesda, MD 20892, (301) 496-7344.

[390] NATIONAL CENTER FOR ATMOSPHERIC RESEARCH

ELIGIBILITY: Summer Employment Program for minority undergraduate students interested in the sciences and engineering. Applicants must be undergraduates with at least 60 hours of coursework and be studying physics, math, computer science, meteorology, electrical engineering, chemistry, technical writing, or other physical sciences. Deadline March.
AMOUNT: Varies
CONTACT: NCAR, Human Resources Administrator, P.O. Box 3000, Boulder, CO 80307, (303) 497-8717.

[391] NATIONAL GEM CENTER FELLOWSHIP PROGRAM

ELIGIBILITY: Minority students in master's or Ph.D. programs in engineering or natural sciences at GEM-member universities. Deadline December 1.
AMOUNT: Full-tuition+
CONTACT: Fellowship Programs, The National GEM Center, P.O. Box 537, Notre Dame, IN 46556, (219) 631-5000.

[392] NATIONAL HEART, LUNG & BLOOD INSTITUTE

ELIGIBILITY: Minority Summer Program in Pulmonary Research Program is intended to encourage qualified minority school faculty and graduate students to develop interests in skills in research in pulmonary diseases at established (minority) pulmonary training centers.
AMOUNT: Varies
CONTACT: Program Administrator, National Heart, Lung & Blood Institute, Research Training & Development, Westwood Bldg., Room 640, Bethesda, MD 20892, (301) 496-7668.

[393] NATIONAL HEART, LUNG, & BLOOD INSTITUTE

ELIGIBILITY: Minority School Faculty Development Award. This program is intended to encourage the development of faculty investigators at minority schools in areas relevant to cardiovascular, pulmonary, and hematologic diseases and resources. Candidates should be minority school faculty members who are U.S. citizens, noncitizen nationals or permanent residents, with a doctoral degree or equivalent in a biomedical science.

AMOUNT: Varies

CONTACT: Program Administrator, National Heart, Lung & Blood Institute, National Institutes of Health, Federal Bldg., Room 3C02, Bethesda, MD 20892, (301) 496-1724.

[394] NATIONAL INSTITUTES OF HEALTH RESEARCH APPRENTICE PROGRAM FOR MINORITY HIGH SCHOOL STUDENTS

ELIGIBILITY: Program is designed to stimulate interest among minority high school students in science careers and to establish individualized working relationships between these students and active researchers. Apprentices are paid a salary equivalent to the minimum wage.

AMOUNT: Varies

CONTACT: Program Administrator, National Institutes of Health, Div. of Research Resources, Bldg. 31, Room 5B23, Bethesda, MD 20892, (301) 496-6743.

[395] NATIONAL INSTITUTES OF HEALTH

ELIGIBILITY: Marc Faculty Fellowship Program. Applicants must be faculty members of a public or private nonprofit university, four-year college or other institution offering undergraduate, graduate, or health professional degrees with a substantial minority student enrollment. Institutions nominate faculty members for these fellowships which support either a period of advanced study in research training leading to a graduate degree or a period of post-doctoral research training in the biomedical sciences. Stipends, based upon the applicant's current salary, are not to exceed $25,000 per year. Support is available for periods of up to 3 years at the end of which time the fellow is expected to return to his

or her institution. Deadline January 10, September 10 and May 1.
AMOUNT: Varies
CONTACT: National Institution of General Medical Services, Attn: Dr. Adolphus Toliver, Building 45, Suite SA-37, 45 Center Drive, MSC 6200, Bethesda, MD 20892, (301) 594-3900.

[396] NATIONAL INSTITUTES OF HEALTH

ELIGIBILITY: The Minority Biomedical Research Support Program is aimed towards ensuring ethnic minority groups an equal opportunity to pursue careers in biomedical research. The program provides for academic year and summer salaries and wages for faculty, students, and support personnel needed to conduct a research project. Majors in health science also eligible.
AMOUNT: Varies
CONTACT: National Institutes of Health, Division of Research Resources, Bldg. 31, Room 5B35, Bethesda, MD 20892, (301) 496-6745.

[397] NATIONAL NEWSPAPER PUBLISHERS SCHOLARSHIPS

ELIGIBILITY: Minority college students who wish to pursue careers in journalism.
AMOUNT: $600
CONTACT: National Newspaper Publishers Association, c/o The Louisville Defender, 1720 Dixie Highway, Louisville, KY 40210, (502) 772-2591.

[398] NATIONAL PHARMACEUTICAL FOUNDATION, INC. ETHNIC MINORITY PHARMACY SCHOLARSHIPS

ELIGIBILITY: Applicants must be U.S. citizens majoring in pharmacy. Submission of ACT, SAT, or CEEB scores required.
AMOUNT: $500 to $1,000
CONTACT: President, National Pharmaceutical Foundation, Inc., 1728 17th Street, NE, Washington, DC 20002, (202) 829-5008.

[399] NATIONAL SCHOLARSHIP SERVICE AND FUND FOR MINORITY STUDENTS

ELIGIBILITY: Awards based on need and are designed to supplement the resources of students who have received other aid.
AMOUNT: $200 to $600
CONTACT: National Scholarship Service and Fund for Minority Students, 322 Eighth Avenue, New York, NY 10001.

---

[400] NATIONAL SCIENCE FOUNDATION

ELIGIBILITY: Postdoctoral Fellowships. Scientists and Engineers usually initiate research proposals which are submitted by their employing organizations. Before formal submission, the proposal may be discussed with NSF staff. The foundation considers proposals for support of research in any field of science. The foundation normally will not support clinical research, including research on the etiology, diagnosis, or treatment of physical or mental diseases, abnormality, or malfunction in human beings or animals. Proposals may be submitted by individuals or groups for support of research or research equipment. Research proposals may be submitted at any time. Applicants should allow 6-9 months for review and processing. Contact the foundation for additional information. Applicants must be female and majoring in one of the following: science, atmospheric sciences, chemistry, earth sciences, oceanography, social science, astronomy, biology, computer science/data processing, engineering, materials management/marketing/handling, or physics. Deadline is November 5.
AMOUNT: Varies
CONTACT: Data Support Services Section, National Science Foundation, Nato Postdoctoral Fellowship Directorate for Science/Engineering Education, Washington, DC 20550, (703) 308-5282.

---

[401] NATIONAL SCIENCE FOUNDATION

ELIGIBILITY: Minority Graduate Fellowships. Applicant must be a member of a minority group. Eligibility is limited to those who have not completed more than 20 semester/30 quarter hours, or equivalent, of study in any of the qualifying fields, following completion of their undergraduate degree. No student will be eligible for more than 3 years of any NSF graduate fellowship support. Recipient will be required to enroll in full-time programs leading to graduate degrees in one of the following majors: mathematics, biology, social science, physical science, science, engineering or humanities. Must be a U.S. citizen.

AMOUNT: $12,550

CONTACT: National Research Council, The Fellowship Office, 2101 Constitution Avenue, Washington, DC 20418, (202) 334-2872.

[402] NATIONAL SECURITY AGENCY UNDERGRADUATE TRAINING PROGRAM

ELIGIBILITY: Any student, particularly minority students, who chooses a full-time college major in electrical or computer engineering, computer science, mathematics, or Asian, Middle Eastern, or Slavic languages. Students must attend classes full time and work at NSA during summers. Students must maintain a 3.0 GPA. After graduation, the student must work for NSA for at least one and half times the length of study.

AMOUNT: Full tuition+

CONTACT: NSA, Undergraduate Training Program, Manager, Attn: M322 (UTP), Ft. Meade, MD 20755-6000, (800) 962-9398.

[403] NATIONAL SOCIETY OF PROFESSIONAL ENGINEERS RACIAL MINORITY GRANTS

ELIGIBILITY: Minority or female high school seniors who rank in the top 1/4 of their class, with plans to major in engineering. Financial need required.

AMOUNT: $1,000

CONTACT: National Society of Professional Engineers Education Foundation, 2029 K. Street, NW, Washington, DC 20006, (202) 463-2300.

[404] NATIONAL STUDENT NURSES ASSOCIATION

ELIGIBILITY: Nine scholarships for undergraduate minority students interested in nursing and demonstrating financial need. Deadline February 1; applications available in September.

AMOUNT: $1,000 to $2,500

CONTACT: National Student Nurses Association, 555 West 57th Street, New York, NY 10019, (212) 581-2211.

---

[405] NATIONAL TECHNICAL ASSOCIATION

ELIGIBILITY: Award is for minority students pursuing degrees in finance and engineering. Deadline March 31.
AMOUNT: 50% tuition
CONTACT: Scholarship Officer, National Technical Association, P.O. Box 27787, Washington, DC 20038, (202) 829-6100.

---

[406] NATIONAL URBAN LEAGUE

ELIGIBILITY: Dart & Kraft/National Urban League Scholarship. Awarded to minorities in good scholastic standing. Applicants must be full-time undergraduate juniors pursuing bachelor's degrees in engineering, marketing, manufacturing operations, finance, or business administration at an accredited institution. Deadline April.
AMOUNT: $1,000 to $10,000
CONTACT: Director of Education, National Urban League, 500 East 62nd Street, New York, NY 10021, (213) 310-9000.

---

[407] NAVAL RESERVE OFFICERS TRAINING CORPS (NROTC) SCHOLARSHIP PROGRAM

ELIGIBILITY: Applicants must be U.S. citizens and meet age, physical, personal, and educational requirements outlined by NROTC standards.
AMOUNT: Varies
CONTACT: NROTC, Chief of Naval Education and Training, N21, 250 Dallas Street, Pensacola, FL 32508, (800) NAV-ROTC.

---

[408] NCR FOUNDATION MINORITY SCHOLARSHIP PROGRAM

ELIGIBILITY: Paul Laurence Dunbar Memorial Scholarship. Students should be graduating high school seniors or enrolled in a college-level program. Applicants must be studying accounting, finance, business,

computer science, engineering, or related field.
AMOUNT: $5,000 a year up to four years
CONTACT: College Relations Manager, NCR Corporation, World Headquarters, 1700 S. Patterson Blvd., Dayton, OH 45479, (513) 445-1337.

---

[409] NEBRASKA STUDENT LOAN PROGRAM

ELIGIBILITY: Applicants must show financial need and be enrolled in an eligible school approved by NSLP. Applicants must meet other eligibility criteria; details in the NSLP application.
AMOUNT: Varies
CONTACT: NSLP, P.O. Box 82507, Lincoln, NE 68501-2507, (402) 475-8686.

---

[410] UNIVERSITY OF NEBRASKA, OMAHA
ISAACSON EARLY ENTRY TUITION GRANT

ELIGIBILITY: Omaha high school students. The Isaacson Early Entry Tuition Grant has been established to encourage ethnic minority student participation in the UNO Early Entry Program. The grant will pay full tuition costs for 3 credit hours per semester.
CONTACT: University of Nebraska at Omaha, Office of Financial Aid, Omaha, NE 68182, (402) 554-2327.

---

[411] NEGRO EDUCATIONAL EMERGENCY DRIVE
(NEED)

ELIGIBILITY: Black students attending high school in Pennsylvania and accepted at a college in that state. Geared towards the average student, rather than the top achiever.
AMOUNT: $100 to $500
CONTACT: Negro Educational Emergency Drive, 2003 Law & Finance Bldg., 429 Fourth Avenue, Pittsburgh, PA 15219, (412) 566-2760.

---

[412] NELLIE MAE EXCEL EDUCATION LOANS FOR STUDENTS AND FAMILIES

ELIGIBILITY: Borrower can be a parent, spouse, student, or other responsible person and must be a U.S. citizen or permanent resident and live in the U.S. EXCEL loans are available to students at any accredited institution.
AMOUNT: Loan amounts $2,000 to $20,000 a year
CONTACT: Nellie Mae, Credit Department, 50 Braintree Hill Park, Suite 300, Braintree, MA 02184, (800) 634-9308.

---

[413] NELLIE MAE GRADEXCEL EDUCATION LOANS FOR STUDENTS AND FAMILIES

ELIGIBILITY: GradEXCEL loans are for graduate and professional students and eligibility is based on future earning potential. A student may borrow on his/her own or choose to have a co-borrower who must have a satisfactory credit history and demonstrate sufficient current income. The student or co-borrower must be a U.S. citizen or permanent resident living in the U.S.
AMOUNT: Loan amounts $2,000 to $20,000 a year
CONTACT: Nellie Mae, Credit Department, 50 Braintree Hill Park, Suite 300, Braintree, MA 02184, (800) 634-9308.

---

[414] NELLIE MAE SHARE EDUCATION LOANS FOR STUDENTS AND FAMILIES

ELIGIBILITY: Borrower can be a parent, spouse, student, or other responsible person and must be a U.S. citizen or permanent resident and live in the U.S. SHARE loans may be used at any one of the 32 colleges and universities belonging to the Consortium on Financing Higher Education (COFHE): Amherst, Barnard, Brown, Bryn Mawr, Carleton, Columbia, Cornell, Dartmouth, Duke, Georgetown, Harvard, Johns Hopkins, MIT, Mount Holyoke, Northwestern, Oberlin, Pomona, Princeton, Radcliffe, Rice, Smith, Stanford, Swarthmore, Trinity, University of Chicago, University of Pennsylvania, University of Rochester, Washington University, Wellesley, Wesleyan, Williams College, and Yale.
AMOUNT: Loan amounts $2,000 to $20,000 a year

CONTACT: Nellie Mae, Credit Department, 50 Braintree Hill Park, Suite 300, Braintree, MA 02184, (800) 634-9308.

[415] NELLIE MAE GRADSHARE EDUCATION LOANS FOR STUDENTS AND FAMILIES

ELIGIBILITY: GradSHARE loans are for graduate and professional students and eligibility is based on future earning potential. Loans may be used at any graduate school belonging to the Consortium on Financing Higher Education (see entry 414). A student may borrow on his/her own or have a co-borrower who must have a satisfactory credit history and demonstrate sufficient current income. The student or co-borrower must be a U.S. citizen or permanent resident living in the U.S.
AMOUNT: Loan amounts $2,000 to $15,000 a year
CONTACT: Nellie Mae, Credit Department, 50 Braintree Hill Park, Suite 300, Braintree, MA 02184, (800) 634-9308.

[416] NEW MEXICO INSTITUTE OF MINING AND TECHNOLOGY

ELIGIBILITY: Technical Community Minority Scholarship. Applicant must be a minority majoring in technical communications. Deadline March 1.
AMOUNT: $500
CONTACT: Financial Aid Director, New Mexico Institute of Mining and Technology, Campus Station, Box M, Socorro, NM 87801, (505) 835-5333.

[417] NEW MEXICO STATE UNIVERSITY

ELIGIBILITY: Designated academic opportunity is available to incoming freshman women and minority students. Must be a U.S. citizen, have a 3.0 GPA, and major in engineering.
AMOUNT: Varies
CONTACT: Financial Aid Director, New Mexico State University, Box 5100, Las Cruces, NM 88003, (505) 646-4105.

[418] NEW MEXICO STATE UNIVERSITY
ELIGIBILITY: The TRW Scholarship is available to junior or senior minority students with a 3.0 GPA and majoring in electrical engineering.
AMOUNT: Varies
CONTACT: Dean of Engineering, New Mexico State University, Las Cruces, NM 88003, (505) 646-0111.

[419] NEW MEXICO STATE UNIVERSITY
ELIGIBILITY: National Action Council Award may be renewed until graduation provided the recipient maintains academic requirements. Must be majoring in engineering. Deadline March 1.
AMOUNT: $600 to $800
CONTACT: Dean of Engineering, New Mexico State University, Box 30001, Las Cruces, NM 88003-0001, (505) 646-3547.

[420] NEW MEXICO STATE UNIVERSITY
ELIGIBILITY: Minorities Access to Research. Awarded to under-graduates to prepare for pursuit of a Ph.D. Applicants must have 3.0 GPA and be majoring in biology, chemistry, or medicine. Deadline March 1.
AMOUNT: Varies
CONTACT: New Mexico State University, Box 30001, Department of Biology, Las Cruces, NM 88003-0001, (505) 646-2001.

[421] NEW MEXICO STATE UNIVERSITY
ELIGIBILITY: The Rockwell International Scholarship is awarded to a female or minority student of junior standing. The recipient is chosen by the company on the basis of career potential, scholastic achievement, and need. The award is renewable if the recipient continues to meet the requirements. Must be majoring in one of the following engineering areas: electrical, chemical or mechanical. Must have a 2.8 GPA. Deadline is March 1.
AMOUNT: $800
CONTACT: Dean of Engineering, New Mexico State University, Box 3Z, Las Cruces, NM 88003, (505) 646-0111.

[422] NEWSDAY SCHOLARSHIP COMMITTEE FOR MINORITIES

ELIGIBILITY: Minority student graduating from a high school in Nassau or Suffolk County, New York. Must attend college in the United States. Deadline March 15.
AMOUNT: $5,000
CONTACT: Reggie Tuggle, Newsday, Long Island, NY 11747, (516) 454-2183.

[423] THE NEWSPAPER FUND SCHOLARSHIP/ INTERNSHIP CONTEST

ELIGIBILITY: Gives minority college seniors studying journalism a paid internship at a newspaper or news service specified by the Newspaper Fund. Further, a cash award may be applied to graduate school or to repay undergraduate debt.
AMOUNT: Varies
CONTACT: The Newspaper Fund, P.O. Box 300, Princeton, NJ 08540, (609) 452-2820.

[424] NEW YORK ALLIANCE OF BLACK SCHOOL EDUCATORS

ELIGIBILITY: Gwendolyn Calvert Baker Scholarship for an outstanding, African-American high school senior who plans a career in education.
AMOUNT: $5,000
CONTACT: Fund for Educational Excellence, c/o NYABSE, Attn: Dr. Gwendolyn C. Baker Humanitarian Scholarship Award, P.O. Box 604, Bronx, NY 10462.

[425] NEW YORK STATE DEPARTMENT OF EDUCATION REGENTS PROFESSIONAL OPPORTUNITY SCHOLARSHIPS

ELIGIBILITY: Priority given to disadvantaged and underrepresented populations. Must be majoring in one of the following areas: chiropractic medicine, optometry, podiatry, veterinary medicine, dental hygiene, physical therapy or medical technology. Financial need required.

AMOUNT: $1,000 to $5,000
CONTACT: Professional Opportunity Scholarship Administration, NYS Dept. of Education, Professional Education Testing Bureau, Cultural Education Center, Albany, NY 12230, (518) 474-6394.

[426] NEW YORK UNIVERSITY
ELIGIBILITY: AEJ/NYU Summer Intern Program for Minorities in Journalism. This is a ten-week internship program in which students are placed in entry-level positions at magazines, newspapers, book publishers, broadcasting stations and corporate public relations departments. Interns work 35 hours per week and are paid minimum weekly salaries of $175-$200. Interns participate in the two-credit course "Journalism and Minorities" and on-site visits. Housing is available on the New York University campus for a fee. Deadline December 17.
AMOUNT: Varies
CONTACT: Institute of Afro-American Affairs, New York University, 269 Mercer Street, Suite 601, New York, NY 10003, (212) 598-7095.

[427] NEW YORK UNIVERSITY
ELIGIBILITY: Martin Luther King, Jr., Scholarship Program. Full-tuition scholarships for four years, for minority or economically disadvantaged students who exemplify the ideals of Martin Luther King, Jr., and who have demonstrated significant academic excellence and achievement. Applicants should show evidence of a commitment to community service, humanitarianism, and social progress. Apply for admission by February 1 and file a financial aid form with college scholarship service by February 15.
CONTACT: Office of Admissions, New York University, P.O. Box 909, Cooper Station, New York, NY 10276, (212) 998-4544.

[428] NIAID MINORITY RESEARCH ENHANCEMENT AWARD
ELIGIBILITY: The National Institute of Allergy and Infectious Diseases provides support for underrepresented minority researchers. Must be majoring in biomedical research.

AMOUNT: Varies
CONTACT: Chief, Research Manpower Development, National Institutes of Health, Westwood Bldg., Room 7A03, NIAID, Bethesda, MD 20892, (301) 496-3461.

---

[429] NISSAN SCHOLARSHIP PROGRAM
ELIGIBILITY: An innovative college scholarship program to help minority students in automotive careers. Applicants must attend universities participating in the program: Northwood University, Midland University, University of Michigan and Xavier University, New Orleans.
AMOUNT: $10,000
CONTACT: Paul Strawhecker, Northwood University, (313) 837-4200 or Clarence Jupiter, Xavier University, (504) 486-7411; or Nissan Division, Public Relations Department, P.O. Box 191, Gardena, CA 90248-0191, (310) 719-5631.

---

[430] NORFOLK STATE UNIVERSITY
ELIGIBILITY: The Delta Sigma Theta—Chesapeake Chapter Scholarship is offered to local black entering students with a GPA of 3.0. This award is renewable for three years.
AMOUNT: $1,000
CONTACT: Norfolk State University, Delta Sigma Theta—Chesapeake Chapter, Norfolk, VA 23504, (804) 623-8229.

---

[431] NORFOLK STATE UNIVERSITY
ELIGIBILITY: Dozoretz National Institute Minority in Science Award. Full tuition and a computer awarded to minorities to increase the number of minority doctors and scientists. This award is renewable for four years. Must be majoring in one of the following: computer science, science or chemistry.
AMOUNT: Varies
CONTACT: Norfolk State University, Admissions Office, Norfolk, VA 23504, (804) 623-8396.

---

[432] NORTH CAROLINA COMMUNITY COLLEGE SCHOLARSHIP PROGRAM

ELIGIBILITY: Each school selects its own recipients from applicants. Student must be a N.C. resident enrolled at least part-time at one of the 58 institutions in the community college system. Financial need required, Minority students enrolled in college transferable curriculum programs, persons seeking new job skills, women in non-traditional curricula, and students who participated in an ABE, GED, or H.S. diploma program.
AMOUNT: $400
CONTACT: Scholarship Administrator, Dept. of Community Colleges, 177 Education Bldg., Raleigh, NC 27603, (919) 733-3652.

[433] NORTHEASTERN UNIVERSITY

ELIGIBILITY: The Ralph J. Bunche Scholarship is awarded for 5 years, and totals full tuition for the first year and 1/2 tuition for remaining 4 years. Eligibility is based on academic achievement as determined by the applicant's high school record, class rank, college board examination scores, and letters of recommendation from guidance counselors and teachers.
CONTACT: Northeastern University, 360 Huntington Avenue, Boston, MA 02115, (617) 437-2200.

[434] NORTHEASTERN UNIVERSITY

ELIGIBILITY: Minority Engineering Education Effort. Must be majoring in one of the following engineering areas: chemical, electrical, mechanical, civil or industrial. Financial need required. Deadline May 1.
AMOUNT: $250 to $2,500
CONTACT: Financial Aid Director, Northeastern University, 360 Huntington Avenue, Boston, MA 02115, (617) 437-2200.

[435] NORTHEASTERN STATE UNIVERSITY

ELIGIBILITY: W. W. Keeler Scholarship. Junior year minority students are nominated by the university's faculty and employees. Selection is based on academic achievement. Award is $500 for the junior year and $750 for the senior year if satisfactory academic progress in maintained. Selected students get summer employment opportunities with Phillips Petroleum Company. Applicants must have a 3.0 GPA and be majoring in accounting, journalism, marketing/sales/retailing or science. **CONTACT:** Dean of Student Affairs, Northeastern State University, Tahlequah, OK 74464, (918) 456-5511.

[436] NORTHERN VIRGINIA BRANCH WASHINGTON URBAN LEAGUE, ESSAY

ELIGIBILITY: This essay contest is open to residents of the Northern Virginia area. Participants must be entering college freshmen who will be attending an accredited institution of higher learning in the fall following high school graduation. Awards are payable to the school. Essays must be between 500 and 1,000 words; be typewritten and double spaced or legibly handwritten; be accompanied by entry blank, letter of acceptance from the college or university, high school transcript, and activity form. Essays will be judged for content, originality, organization, style, grammar, spelling, and neatness. Academic standing is also given consideration. Contact the following address for the assigned topic and additional information.
AMOUNT: $1,000
CONTACT: Deputy Director, Northern Virginia Branch, Washington Urban League, Inc., 901 N. Washington Street, #202, Alexandria, VA 22314.

[437] UNIVERSITY OF NORTH FLORIDA

ELIGIBILITY: The Eartha M.M. White Scholarship is awarded to the top entering black students who have a minimum 3.0 GPA and rank in the top 15% of their high school class. Students who have a minimum SAT combined score of 1,000 or a minimum ACT composite score of 23 and have a 3.0 GPA are encouraged to apply. Applicants must submit at least one letter of recommendation from a teacher or counselor and a one-page essay explaining why they want a college education. Deadline March 1.
AMOUNT: $1,000
CONTACT: University of North Florida, Attn: Scholarship Coordinator, 4567 St. Johns Bluff Road, S. Jacksonville, FL 32216, (904) 646-2604.

[438] UNIVERSITY OF NORTH FLORIDA

ELIGIBILITY: The Clayton Hawkins Scholarship is available to an entering black freshman on the basis of outstanding academic and leadership achievement. Must be in the upper 1/5 of class.
AMOUNT: $1,000
CONTACT: University of North Florida, 4567 St. Johns Bluff Road, S. Jacksonville, FL 32216, (904) 646-2604.

[439] NORTHSIDE ASSOCIATION FOR EDUCATIONAL ADVANCEMENT SCHOLARSHIP

ELIGIBILITY: While no requirement is made regarding major or career plans, it is expected that the applicant will be goal-directed and able to discuss their goals during the interview portion of the requirements. These awards are for minority students in Kalamazoo County schools. They are automatically renewed annually if the recipient maintains grades. Contact the high school guidance/counseling office for more information. Must have a 2.0 GPA and financial need required. Deadline April 15.
AMOUNT: $1,300
CONTACT: Local High School Counselors, Northside Association for Educational Advancement, Kalamazoo, MI 49008, (616) 775-0960.

[440] NORTHWEST MISSOURI STATE UNIVERSITY

ELIGIBILITY: Martin Luther King, Jr., Scholarship. Awarded to a full-time minority student with a 3.25 GPA.
AMOUNT: Varies
CONTACT: Northwest Missouri State University, Attn: Scholarship Committee, 800 University Drive, Maryville, MO 64468-6001, (800) 633-1175.

[441] NORTHWEST MISSOURI STATE UNIVERSITY

ELIGIBILITY: Minority Achievement Scholarship. Awarded to minority student with a 2.0 GPA, in the upper 2/5 of their class, and a 21 ACT score. Deadline May 1.
AMOUNT: $1,000 to $1,250
CONTACT: Northwest Missouri State University, Attn: Scholarship

Committee, 800 University Drive, Maryville, MO 64468-6001, (800) 633-1175.

[442] NORTHWEST MISSOURI STATE UNIVERSITY

ELIGIBILITY: Minority Transfer Scholarship. Awarded to a full-time minority transfer student with a 2.7 GPA.
AMOUNT: $1,000 to $1,250
CONTACT: Northwest Missouri State University, Attn: Scholarship Committee, 800 University Drive, Maryville, MO 64468-6001, (800) 633-1175.

[443] NORTHWOOD INSTITUTE

ELIGIBILITY: Chrysler Corp. Minority Scholarship. Relatives of dealers/employees of Chrysler are ineligible. Applicants must be majoring in automotive industry, have a 3.0 GPA, and show financial need.
AMOUNT: $5,000
CONTACT: Private Donor Scholarship Office, Northwood Institute, 3225 Cook Road, Midland, MI 48640-2398, (517) 832-4279.

[444] UNIVERSITY OF NOTRE DAME

ELIGIBILITY: Available scholarships include the Martin Luther King Scholarship Program to assist minority students in financial need.
AMOUNT: $500 to $1,900
CONTACT: Office of Admissions, University of Notre Dame, Notre Dame, IN 46556, (219) 239-6011.

[445] NOVA UNIVERSITY

ELIGIBILITY: The School of Psychology Scholarship for new, continuing and minority M.S., Ph.D., Psy.D. levels with financial need and minimum 3.0 GPA.
AMOUNT: $1,500 to $2,000
CONTACT: Financial Planning Counselor, Nova University, 3301 College Avenue, Ft. Lauderdale, FL 33314, (305) 475-7411.

[446] NOVA UNIVERSITY

ELIGIBILITY: Nova College Honors Award. For day program, freshman with SAT combined score of 1,000 or ACT composite score of 22, and transfer and minority students with a 3.0 GPA and 15 or more semester credits from a regionally accredited institution.
AMOUNT: Varies
CONTACT: Financial Planning Counselor, Nova University, 3301 College Avenue, Ft. Lauderdale, FL 33314, (305) 475-7411.

[447] NURSES' EDUCATIONAL FUND

ELIGIBILITY: The Estelle Massey Osborne Scholarship and the M. Elizabeth Carnegie Scholarship. Applicants must be black registered nurses pursuing a master's or doctoral degree program, must attend a National League for Nursing program, and must be a member of a professional nursing program. Deadline February.
AMOUNT: $2,500 to $10,000
CONTACT: Nurses' Educational Fund, 555 West 57 Street, New York, NY 10019, (212) 582-8820.

[448] NYACK COLLEGE

ELIGIBILITY: The Tom Skinner Associates Scholarship is available to black entering freshman who have a 3.0 GPA and financial need. Deadline March 1.
AMOUNT: Varies
CONTACT: Nyack College, South Boulevard, Nyack, NY 10960, (914) 358-1710.

[449] OAK RIDGE ASSOCIATED UNIVERSITIES

ELIGIBILITY: Historically Black Colleges and Universities Nuclear Energy Training Program for Undergraduates. Applicants must be undergraduate students seeking degrees in nuclear energy-related areas at designated historically black colleges and universities. Applicants must be either U.S. citizens or permanent residents. Deadline February.
AMOUNT: $6,000+ per year

CONTACT: Oak Ridge Associated Universities, P.O. Box 117, Oak Ridge, TN 37831-0117, (615) 576-3428.

---

[450] OAKWOOD COLLEGE

ELIGIBILITY: Must be a black entering freshman and have a strong academic background. Apply early.
AMOUNT: $1,000 to $2,000
CONTACT: Oakwood College, Huntsville, AL 35896, (205) 837-1630.

---

[451] OHIO NORTHERN UNIVERSITY

ELIGIBILITY: Minority Engineering Scholarship is awarded to minority students majoring in one of the following engineering areas: civil, mechanical or electrical. Deadline August 21.
AMOUNT: $500 to $2,500
CONTACT: Financial Aid Director, Ohio Northern University, Ada, OH 45810, (419) 772-2272.

---

[452] OKLAHOMA STATE UNIVERSITY

ELIGIBILITY: Minority U.S. citizens are eligible for awards if they have the minimum ACT composite score required for admission and a 3.0 GPA or better on a six or seven semester transcript. Minority applicants who meet the criteria described for other scholarships will qualify for the highest award.
AMOUNT: $725
CONTACT: University Scholarship Director, Oklahoma State University, Hanner/Whitehurst Hall, Student Union, Stillwater, OK 74078, (405) 744-7541.

---

[453] UNIVERSITY OF OKLAHOMA

ELIGIBILITY: Graduate Assistantships from the College of Arts and Sciences Office of Minority Participation. Applicants must be U.S. citizens, must hold a bachelor's or master's degree and must show strong promise of successfully completing a graduate degree program, must be leading to a master's or doctoral degree in the humanities, social sciences,

mathematical, physical, or biological sciences, library and information sciences, social work, or history and philosophy of science. Deadline April.
AMOUNT: $7,500 to $12,000
CONTACT: Assistant Dean, College of Arts and Sciences, Room 110C, University of Oklahoma, Norman, OK 73019-0315, (800) 522-0772 in state, (800) 523-7363 out of state.

---

[454] UNIVERSITY OF OKLAHOMA
ELIGIBILITY: Minority Achievement Awards are available to entering minority students on the basis of grades, test scores, activities, and leadership skills. Must have a 3.0 GPA.
AMOUNT: $750
CONTACT: Financial Aid Director, University of Oklahoma, 731 Elm, Robertson AKK, Norman, OK 73019, (405) 325-2151.

---

[455] OLD DOMINION UNIVERSITY
ELIGIBILITY: Holland Dunston Ellis, Jr. Memorial Scholarship. Awarded to a minority student who resides in Virginia.
AMOUNT: Varies
CONTACT: Old Dominion University, Office of Student Financial Aid, 121 Rollins Hall, Norfolk, VA 23529-0052, (804) 683-3683.

---

[456] OLD DOMINION UNIVERSITY
ELIGIBILITY: The Martin Luther King, Jr., Scholarship is awarded to a black student majoring in engineering, accounting, or technology. Financial need is required. Applicants must have completed at least 60 credit hours.
AMOUNT: $1,000
CONTACT: Mary Schultz, Office of Student Financial Aid, Old Dominion University, 121 Rollins Hall, Norfolk, VA 23529, (804) 683-3683.

---

[457] OLD DOMINION UNIVERSITY
ELIGIBILITY: Vice Admiral Samuel L. Gravely Scholarship is awarded to entering black students active in ROTC. The recipient will participate in the Hampton Roads NROTC program at ODU, but will not receive a NROTC scholarship for the award year.
AMOUNT: Varies
CONTACT: Mary Schultz, Office of Student Financial Aid, Old Dominion University, 121 Rollins Hall, Norfolk, VA 23529, (804) 683-3683.

[458] OLD DOMINION UNIVERSITY
ELIGIBILITY: The Herman E. Valentine Scholarships. Qualified recipients must be black, graduate students preferably attending ODU part time. A minimum of three scholarships are to be awarded for those majoring in business administration/management, computer science and/or data processing and engineering, for two semesters at six credit hours each semester.
AMOUNT: Up to $5,000
CONTACT: Mary Schultz, Office of Student Financial Aid, Old Dominion University, 121 Rollins Hall, Norfolk, VA 23529, (804) 683-3683.

[459] OLD DOMINION UNIVERSITY
ELIGIBILITY: The Edgar and Kathleen Kovner Scholarship Awards are based on student's potential to successfully complete the requirements for a bachelor's degree. All recipients must be full-time students, and can be entering freshmen, transfer or continuing undergraduates. Must be majoring in engineering or technology.
AMOUNT: $500
CONTACT: Mary Schultz, Office of Student Financial Aid, Old Dominion University, 121 Rollins Hall, Norfolk, VA 23529, (804) 683-3683.

[460] OLD DOMINION UNIVERSITY
ELIGIBILITY: Special Minority Part-Time Tuition Grants are funded through gifts to the institution to assist minority students enrolling in graduate programs for the first time. Grants cover part-time tuition.
AMOUNT: Part-time tuition

CONTACT: Mary Schultz, Office of Student Financial Aid, Old Dominion University, 121 Rollins Hall, Norfolk, VA 23529, (804) 683-3683.

[461] OLD DOMINION UNIVERSITY

ELIGIBILITY: Alfred B. Rollins, Jr., Scholarship Recipient will be a minority student who is a rising senior with financial need and a 2.5 GPA.
AMOUNT: $1,000
CONTACT: Mary Schultz, Office of Student Financial Aid, Old Dominion University, 121 Rollins Hall, Norfolk, VA 23529, (804) 683-3683.

[462] OMEGA PSI PHI FRATERNITY, INC.

ELIGIBILITY: The chapters nominate a district scholar who is a college senior with at least a 3.0 GPA. The winner receives a matching dollar amount from the Drew commission. Applicants must be an active member of Omega Psi Phi and demonstrate financial need.
AMOUNT: Up to $500
CONTACT: Omega Psi Phi Fraternity, Inc., International Headquarters, 2714 Georgia Avenue, NW, Washington, DC 20001, (202) 667-7158.

[463] OMEGA PSI PHI FRATERNITY, INC.

ELIGIBILITY: The Graduate and Undergraduate Scholarship Grants are for black males active in Omega Psi Phi. Deadlines for undergraduate applications are October 15th and May 15th annually. Deadline for graduate application is May 15th annually.
AMOUNT: $500
CONTACT: Omega Psi Phi Fraternity, Inc., International Headquarters, 2714 Georgia Avenue, NW, Washington, DC 20001, (202) 667-7158.

[464] OMEGA PSI PHI FRATERNITY, INC.

ELIGIBILITY: The Creative and Research Fellowship is awarded to help those scholars and creative artists who need financial assistance to complete a work that is already in progress or to publish a manuscript of study which has been completed. This is for black males that have completed their sophomore year majoring in one of the following:

humanities, natural sciences, education, physical science, or social science. Must be an active Omega Psi Phi member.
AMOUNT: $1,000
CONTACT: Omega Psi Phi Fraternity, Inc., International Headquarters, 2714 Georgia Avenue, NW, Washington, DC 20001, (202) 667-7158.

---

[465] OMEGA PSI PHI FRATERNITY, INC.
ELIGIBILITY: Founders' Memorial Scholarships. Applicants must be active in the Omega Psi Phi Fraternity, have a 3.0 GPA and show financial need. Extracurricular activities and community/campus involvement required. Award is not available to freshman, but this information may be used for planning purposes.
AMOUNT: $300
CONTACT: Omega Psi Phi Fraternity, Inc., International Headquarters, 2714 Georgia Avenue, NW, Washington, DC 20001, (202) 667-7158.

---

[466] OMEGA PSI PHI DADE COUNTY BLACK MALE AWARD
ELIGIBILITY: Awarded to a black male student entering college with a 2.7 GPA. Applicant must be a resident of Dade County, Florida, and must be nominated by a fraternity member. Deadline February 2.
AMOUNT: $1,000
CONTACT: Omega Psi Phi Fraternity, Inc., Attn: Scholarship Chairman, 13121 NW 18th Avenue, Miami, FL 33167.

---

[467] OMEGA WIVES SCHOLARSHIP
ELIGIBILITY: Applicants must be black females who are William Penn High seniors and who have maintained an 80% average in grades 10-12. A transcript must accompany application. Applicants must have participated in school and/or community related activities and be accepted by an accredited school of higher learning. Contact your high school guidance counselor for further information and an application form.
AMOUNT: Varies
CONTACT: William Penn High School, Broad and Master Streets, Philadelphia, PA 19122.

[468] OTTERBEIN COLLEGE

ELIGIBILITY: Ammons-Thomas Minority Scholarship. Awarded to a minority student with a 2.5 GPA, in the upper 3/5 of his or her class. Applicant must be a U.S. citizen. Deadline May 1.
AMOUNT: $1,500
CONTACT: Otterbein College, Attn: Financial Aid Director, West College Avenue and Grove Street, Westerville, OH 43081, (614) 823-1500.

[469] UNIVERSITY OF THE PACIFIC

ELIGIBILITY: Must be majoring in one of the following engineering areas: civil, mechanical, computer, electrical, systems or physics. Financial need required.
AMOUNT: $250 to $2,500
CONTACT: Financial Aid Director, University of the Pacific, Stockton, CA 95211, (209) 946-3091.

[470] PACIFIC GAS & ELECTRIC COMPANY

ELIGIBILITY: There are 2 awards for $1,000 a year for four years and 4 one-time awards for $1,000. The applicant must be a deserving minority high school senior who has advanced despite economic, cultural, or motivational disadvantages. The applicant must reside or attend school in the Pacific Gas & Electric Company service area. Applications may be obtained from high school guidance counselors. Deadline November 15.
CONTACT: Pacific Gas & Electric Company, 77 Beale Street, Room F-1500, San Francisco, CA 94106, (415) 972-1338.

[471] PATRICIA ROBERTS HARRIS FELLOWSHIP

ELIGIBILITY: Must plan a career in agricultural education. Must be a minority student with a 3.2 GPA. Financial need required.
AMOUNT: $8,000
CONTACT: Chair, Agriculture Education Dept., Iowa State University, 201 Curtiss Hall, Ames, IA 50011, (515) 294-0241.

[472] PEIRCE JUNIOR COLLEGE
ELIGIBILITY: ARA Services Scholarship is available to a second year, minority student majoring in a discipline that would be employable at ARA, Inc. Must have a 3.0 GPA. Awards are based primarily on academic achievement and contribution to Peirce Junior College. Deadline end of Spring Semester.
AMOUNT: Varies
CONTACT: Financial Aid Director, Peirce Junior College, 1420 Pine Street, Philadelphia, PA 19102, (215) 545-6400.

[473] UNIVERSITY OF PENNSYLVANIA
ELIGIBILITY: Gloria Twine Chisum Scholarship awarded to a black full-time student majoring in social work who shows need and merit.
AMOUNT: $2,000
CONTACT: University of Pennsylvania, Attn: School of Social Work, Admissions Office, 3701 Locust Walk, Philadelphia, PA 19104-6214, (215) 898-5539.

[474] UNIVERSITY OF PENNSYLVANIA
ELIGIBILITY: Louise P. Shoemaker Award to a full-time minority student majoring in social work.
AMOUNT: $2,000
CONTACT: University of Pennsylvania, Attn: School of Social Work, Admissions Office, 3701 Locust Walk, Philadelphia, PA 19104-6214, (215) 898-5539.

[475] UNIVERSITY OF PENNSYLVANIA MINORITY SCHOLARSHIP FUND
ELIGIBILITY: Awarded to full-time minority students who are majoring in social work and who show need and merit.
AMOUNT: $1,000 to $8,000
CONTACT: Universityof Pennsylvania, Attn: School of Social Work, Admissions Office, 3701 Locust Walk, Philadelphia, PA 19104-6214, (215) 898-5539.

[476] PEPPERDINE UNIVERSITY
ELIGIBILITY: Getty Scholarship—for black students preparing for elementary education positions in predominantly minority schools.
AMOUNT: Varies
CONTACT: Office of Admissions, Pepperdine University, Los Angeles, CA 90044, (213) 456-4391.

[477] PHI BETA SIGMA FRATERNITY
ELIGIBILITY: Scholarships, employment referrals, and other programs are available to college-bound black high school students.
AMOUNT: Varies
CONTACT: Phi Beta Sigma Fraternity, Inc., 1327 R Street, NW, Washington, DC 20011, (202) 726-5434.

[478] PHI DELTA KAPPA
ELIGIBILITY: Scholarships available to minority high school seniors who are planning a career in teaching. Deadline January 31.
AMOUNT: Varies
CONTACT: Howard D. Hill, Director of Chapter Programs, Phi Delta Kappa, P.O. Box 789, Bloomington, IN 47402-0789, (812) 339-1156.

[479] PINE MANOR COLLEGE
ELIGIBILITY: The Massachusetts Minority Scholarship is available to minority residents of Massachusetts on the basis of academic ability and record, commitment to a liberal arts education, recommendations from three adults, and a personal interview with one or more faculty members at the college. The award provides full tuition. Deadline March 1.
AMOUNT: Varies
CONTACT: Financial Aid Director, Pine Manor College, 400 Heath Street, Chestnut Hill, MA 02107, (617) 731-7000.

[480] UNIVERSITY OF PITTSBURGH
ELIGIBILITY: Mellon Grant for NSSFMS Students—for students who have already received aid from the National Scholarship Service and Fund

for Minority Students.
AMOUNT: Varies
CONTACT: Office of Admissions, University of Pittsburgh, Pittsburgh, PA 15260-0001, (412) 624-4141.

---

[481] UNIVERSITY OF PITTSBURGH

ELIGIBILITY: General Studies Grants; for minority and disadvantaged students entering the School of General Studies.
AMOUNT: Max. cost of tuition
CONTACT: Office of Admissions, University of Pittsburgh, Pittsburgh, PA 15260-0001, (412) 624-4141.

---

[482] UNIVERSITY OF PITTSBURGH

ELIGIBILITY: The Challenge Scholarship is for black students on basis of high school academics/entrance exams. Applicants must be in the upper 2/5 of their class, have a minimum 3.0 GPA and show financial need. Must be majoring in liberal arts or humanities.
AMOUNT: $1,000 to $4,000
CONTACT: University of Pittsburgh, Financial Aid Office, 3rd Floor, Bruce Hall, Pittsburgh, PA 15260, (412) 624-7488.

---

[483] PORTLAND STATE UNIVERSITY

ELIGIBILITY: The Martin Luther King, Jr., Scholarship Fund of Oregon provides support to minority students with high grade point averages studying at any Oregon college.
AMOUNT: Varies
CONTACT: Martin Luther King, Jr., Scholarship Fund of Oregon, Portland State University, P.O. Box 751, Portland, OR 97207.

---

[484] UNIVERSITY OF PORTLAND

ELIGIBILITY: King-Kennedy Scholarship; for minority students.
AMOUNT: Varies
CONTACT: Office of Admissions, University of Portland, 5000 N. Willamette Blvd., Portland, OR 97203-5798, (503) 283-7911.

[485] POTOMAC VALLEY ALUMNAE CHAPTER

ELIGIBILITY: Alum-Delta Sigma Theta Scholarship. This is for an entering black student demonstrating financial need. This scholarship is renewable for four years. Students may be recommended by their high school. Deadline March 31.
AMOUNT: $2,000
CONTACT: Potomac Valley Alumnae Chapter, Delta Sigma Theta Sorority, Inc., Attn: Scholarship Committee, 9913 Sorrel Avenue, Potomac, MD 20854, (301) 299-8011.

[486] PROFESSIONAL OPPORTUNITY SCHOLARSHIP

ELIGIBILITY: Applicants must have completed undergraduate work with assistance from HEOP, EOP seek, or College Discovery Opportunity Program. Must major in physical therapy. Financial need required. Deadline June 1.
AMOUNT: Up to $5,000
CONTACT: State Education Department, Cultural Education Center, Empire State Plaza, Albany, NY 12230.

[487] PROVIDENCE COLLEGE

ELIGIBILITY: The Mary J. Benson Scholarship is awarded to deserving black students who can show financial need.
AMOUNT: Varies
CONTACT: Financial Aid Director, Providence College, Providence, RI 02918-0001, (401) 865-2286.

[488] PURDUE UNIVERSITY

ELIGIBILITY: Merit Award for Minorities—given in the freshman year, applicant must be admitted to the school of engineering and have a strong academic background, particularly in math and science.
AMOUNT: Varies
CONTACT: Office of Admissions, Purdue University, West Lafayette, IN 47907, (317) 749-2681.

[489] QUEENS COLLEGE OUTSTANDING MINORITY AWARD

ELIGIBILITY: Awarded to minority students attending Queens College. Deadline February 1.
AMOUNT: Varies
CONTACT: Queens College, Attn: Director of Scholarships, 1900 Selwyn Avenue, Charlotte, NC 28774, (704) 337-2225.

[490] QUINNIPIAC COLLEGE

ELIGIBILITY: Minority Scholarships. Minority students who indicate unusual potential are eligible for this award. This award is renewable with a 2.5 GPA. Deadline March 1.
AMOUNT: $3,500
CONTACT: Financial Aid Director, Quinnipiac College, Mount Carmel Avenue, Hamden, CT 06518-0569, (203) 281-8750.

[491] RACINE ENVIRONMENT COMMITTEE EDUCATIONAL ASSISTANCE PROGRAM

ELIGIBILITY: Minority group members and low-income youths who are residents of Racine and/or graduates of a local high school.
AMOUNT: $100 to $1,000
CONTACT: Racine Environment Committee Educational Fund, 316 Fifth Street, Racine, WI 53403, (414) 637-8893.

[492] RACINE ENVIRONMENT COMMITTEE EDUCATIONAL FUND

ELIGIBILITY: Award is given to a minority and low income student from the city of Racine. Must have a 2.0 GPA. Financial need required. Deadline June 30.
AMOUNT: $1,200
CONTACT: Scholarship Officer, Racine Environment Committee, 310 Fifth Street, Room 101, Racine, WI 53403, (414) 631-5600.

[493] RANDOLPH-MACON COLLEGE

ELIGIBILITY: Offers scholarships ranging from $5,000 to full tuition to outstanding entering black freshman and transfer students. Scholarships, awarded without regard to need, are renewable annually as long as the student maintains the required academic average. Superior academic performance, evidence of strong leadership qualities, and general merit are among the criteria. Recipients may participate in the Honors Program which features special topic courses, students and faculty support groups, organized trips and exclusive use of Pannill (Honors) House.
CONTACT: Office of Admissions, Randolph-Macon College, Ashland, VA 23005, (804) 846-7392.

[494] RANDOLPH-MACON WOMAN'S COLLEGE

ELIGIBILITY: M. Landis Minority Scholarship is awarded to an incoming freshman minority student on the basis of academic record and personal qualities. The award is renewable each year based on committee review. No application is required.
AMOUNT: $2,500
CONTACT: Financial Aid Director, Randolph Macon Woman's College, Lynchburg, VA 24503, (804) 846-7392.

[495] RANDOLPH-MACON WOMAN'S COLLEGE

ELIGIBILITY: The Robert A. and Martha Crocker Spivey Scholarship for minority students. This award is available to entering minority students who are deserving by virtue of academic record and personal qualities. The award is renewable based on committee review. No application is required.
AMOUNT: $2,500
CONTACT: Financial Aid Director, Randolph-Macon Woman's College, Lynchburg, VA 24503, (804) 846-7392.

[496] RED ONION RESTAURANT CORPORATION SCHOLARSHIP

ELIGIBILITY: Offered to women and minorities interested in food services, hotel and restaurant management, business, communications,

and entertainment law who have financial need.
AMOUNT: $500
CONTACT: Red Onion Restaurant Corporation, c/o Human Relations Commission, 200 North Spring Street, 111 City Hall, Los Angeles, CA 90012.

[497] REFORMED CHURCH OF AMERICA
ELIGIBILITY: Minority Education Fund. To minority students admitted to college and RCA members. Financial need required. Deadline is May 15.
AMOUNT: Varies
CONTACT: Reformed Church of America, Office of Human Resources, 475 Riverside Drive, Room 1819, New York, NY 10027, (212) 870-3071.

[498] REGISTERED NURSE FELLOWSHIP PROGRAM FOR ETHNIC/RACIAL MINORITIES
ELIGIBILITY: Fellowship program is for careers in behavioral science research. Applicants must be American citizens or permanent residents. Deadline January 15.
CONTACT: Director, American Nurses Association, Minority Fellowship Programs, 1030 15th Street, NW, Suite 716, Washington, DC 20005, (202) 789-1334.

[499] RENSSELAER POLYTECHNIC INSTITUTE
ELIGIBILITY: International Paper Scholarships for Minorities at Rensselaer offered to freshman minority or female student each year for up to four years who maintain a satisfactory grade point average.
AMOUNT: $2,500 a year
CONTACT: Rensselaer Polytechnic Institute, Office of Minority Student Affairs, Troy, NY 12180-3590, (518) 276-6531.

[500] INTERNATIONAL PAPER TO SUPPORT SCHOLARSHIPS FOR MINORITIES AT RENSSELAER POLYTECHNIC INSTITUTE

ELIGIBILITY: Award to one minority or female student at Rensselaer Polytechnic Institute. Applicants must maintain a satisfactory GPA.
AMOUNT: $2,500
CONTACT: Office of Minority Student Affairs, Rensselaer Polytechnic Institute, Troy, NY 12180, (518) 276-6531.

[501] RHODES COLLEGE

ELIGIBILITY: The National Achievement Scholarships are available to entering freshmen who are finalists in the National Achievement Scholarship program for outstanding Negro students, who have indicated Rhodes College as their first choice college, and who have not been selected as winners of other National Achievement Scholarships.
AMOUNT: $500 to $2,000 dependent upon financial need.
CONTACT: Rhodes College, 2000 North Parkway, Memphis, TN 38112, (901) 274-1800.

[502] RICE UNIVERSITY

ELIGIBILITY: Rice Minority Scholarship Program. Minority students seeking enrollment at Rice University are eligible. Applicants must exhibit outstanding qualifications and ability academically and non-academically. Deadline January 15.
AMOUNT: Varies
CONTACT: Ron Moss, Director of Admissions, Rice University, P.O. Box 1892, Houston, TX 77251, (800) 527-6957.

[503] RICK DAVIS SCHOLARSHIP

ELIGIBILITY: This is awarded to a minority student. Student must take ACT, file FFS and submit UNO Scholarship Application by December 1. This scholarship is 3 years renewable and includes room and board.
AMOUNT: Full tuition
CONTACT: University of Nebraska at Omaha, Office of Financial Aid, 60th & Dodge Street, Omaha, NE 68182, (402) 554-2327.

[504] RIDER COLLEGE

ELIGIBILITY: Offers full-tuition minority scholarships. Up to 25 scholarships are given each year to students who demonstrate academic excellence as evidenced by grades, strength of academic program, SAT scores, and rank in class.
CONTACT: Barry Taylor, Assistant Director of Admissions, 2083 Lawrenceville Road, Lawrenceville, NJ 08648-3099, (609) 896-5041.

[505] RIDER COLLEGE MINORITY TRANSFER SCHOLARSHIP PROGRAM

ELIGIBILITY: Awarded to minority transfer students based on interview, essay, academic record, and motivation. Deadline August 1.
AMOUNT: Varies
CONTACT: Rider College, Attn: Office of Admissions and Financial Aid, 2083 Lawrenceville Road, Lawrenceville, NJ 08648-3099, (609) 896-5041.

[506] ROANOKE-CHOWAN COMMUNITY COLLEGE

ELIGIBILITY: The Intern Program is available to black sophomores with a GPA of 2.0. Financial need is required.
AMOUNT: $100
CONTACT: Roanoke-Chowan Community College, Route 2, Box 46-A, Ahoskie, NC 27910, (919) 332-5921.

[507] ROBERT WOOD JOHNSON FOUNDATION

ELIGIBILITY: The Foundation funds will be used for need-based scholarships to first and second year medical students.
AMOUNT: $1,000 to $5,000
CONTACT: The Robert Wood Johnson Foundation, College Road, P.O. Box 2316, Princeton, NJ 08543-2316, (609) 452-8701.

[508] ROBERTS WESLEYAN COLLEGE

ELIGIBILITY: Minority Student Scholarships for full-time minority students who are U.S. citizens or permanent residents with financial need

and who exhibit academic achievement and leadership qualities. Must have a 3.0 GPA. Deadline May 1.
AMOUNT: $500
CONTACT: Director of Financial Aid, Roberts Wesleyan College, 2301 Westside Drive, Rochester, NY 14624-1997, (716) 594-9471.

---

[509] ROCKHURST COLLEGE

ELIGIBILITY: Special Minority Scholarships based on merit and not on need to talented black, Hispanic and other minority men and women.
AMOUNT: Varies
CONTACT: Rockhurst College, 5225 Troost Avenue, Kansas City, MO 64110-2599, (816) 926-4100.

---

[510] ROLLINS COLLEGE MINORITY STUDENT SCHOLARSHIPS

ELIGIBILITY: The Martin Luther King, Jr., Scholarship. This scholarship competition requires a separate application and essay.
AMOUNT: $3,000 annually
CONTACT: Office/Student Financial Planning, Rollins College, Campus Box 2721, Winter Park, FL 32789-4499, (407) 646-2395.

---

[511] ROLLINS COLLEGE

ELIGIBILITY: The William Randolph Hearst Scholarship is awarded annually to an entering minority freshman. No application required.
AMOUNT: $1,500
CONTACT: Financial Aid Director, Rollins College, Campus Box 2721, Winter Park, FL 32789, (305) 646-2173.

---

[512] ROSEMONT COLLEGE OPPORTUNITY GRANT

ELIGIBILITY: Awarded to minority students who have overcome significant historical, educational, and economic hardship to pursue higher education. Must be a female, a U.S. citizen or a permanent resident. Deadline February 1.
AMOUNT: $7,500

CONTACT: Rosemont College, Attn: Director of Admissions, Rosemont, PA 19010, (610) 527-9721.

[513] ROSS UNIVERSITY SCHOOL OF MEDICINE AND SCHOOL OF VETERINARY MEDICINE IN THE WEST INDIES

ELIGIBILITY: Offers partial scholarships to qualified applicants who want to pursue careers in medicine or veterinary science.
AMOUNT: Varies
CONTACT: Dr. Robert Ross, Chairman of the Board of Trustees, Ross University, 460 West 34th Street, 12th Floor, New York, NY 10001, (212) 279-5500.

[514] RUTGERS UNIVERSITY

ELIGIBILITY: Awards James Dickson Carr Minority Merit Scholarships to black and Puerto Rican students in the top 40% of their high school class who have combined SAT scores of approximately 1,100 or higher. In the three previous years, 125 students have received the awards, worth $5,000 this year. Carr, in 1886, was the first African-American graduate of Rutgers, the eighth oldest college in the country.
AMOUNT: Room, board, tuition and fees total $6,094 for New Jersey residents and $9,500 for out-of-state students.
CONTACT: Mr. James Ruffin, c/o Office of Undergraduate Admissions, Davidson Road, Rutgers University, Piscataway/New Brunswick, NJ 08854, (908) 445-3777.

[515] SACHS FOUNDATION UNDERGRADUATE SCHOLARSHIPS

ELIGIBILITY: Black Colorado residents with at least a 3.6 GPA. Applicants must show community involvement. Deadline March 1.
AMOUNT: $3,000 to $4,000 renewable
CONTACT: Sachs Foundation, 90 S. Cascade Avenue, Suite 1410, Colorado Springs, CO 80903.

[516] SAGINAW VALLEY STATE COLLEGE
ELIGIBILITY: Minority Scholarships renewable by maintaining a 3.0 GPA. Deadline March 1.
AMOUNT: $1,000
CONTACT: Director of Admissions, Saginaw Valley State College, 2250 Pierce Road, University Center, MI 48710, (517) 790-4000.

---

[517] UNIVERSITY OF SAN FRANCISCO
ELIGIBILITY: Bank of America Scholarships are awarded to minority undergraduate business students.
AMOUNT: Varies
CONTACT: Financial Aid Director, University of San Francisco, Champion Hall, Ignatian Heights, San Francisco, CA 94117-1080, (415) 666-6886.

---

[518] SAN FRANCISCO STATE UNIVERSITY
ELIGIBILITY: Scholarships for Underrepresented Minority Students. Offered to students at the undergraduate and MBA level in the College of Business.
AMOUNT: Varies
CONTACT: Sharon Collins, Assistant Dean, College of Business, San Francisco State University, 1600 Holloway Avenue, San Francisco, CA 94132, (415) 338-6363, fax: (415) 338-6237.

---

[519] SANGAMON STATE UNIVERSITY
ELIGIBILITY: Illinois Association Community Action Scholarship is available to a minority student planning a career in public affairs on the basis of need.
AMOUNT: $300
CONTACT: Sangamon State University, Springfield, IL 62708, (217) 786-6600.

---

[520] SANGAMON STATE UNIVERSITY

ELIGIBILITY: The William Ferris Cummings Award is available to an undergraduate or graduate student who is a member of a minority group and interested in community service. The recipient should be in good academic standing and have demonstrated financial need. Majors: social science, education, social work, and political science. Deadline April 1.
AMOUNT: $100 to $200
CONTACT: Financial Aid Director, Sangamon State University, Springfield, IL 62708, (217) 786-6600.

[521] SANGAMON STATE UNIVERSITY

ELIGIBILITY: The Otis Morgan Memorial Scholarship is available to a minority student who plans to teach. Financial need required. Deadline April 1.
AMOUNT: $250
CONTACT: Financial Aid Director, Sangamon State University, Springfield, IL 62708, (217) 786-6600.

[522] SAN JOAQUIN DELTA COLLEGE

ELIGIBILITY: The Links Incorporated Scholarship is for black females in their freshman or sophomore year. This is available to students who have completed at least one semester as a full-time student with a minimum GPA of 3.0.
AMOUNT: Varies
CONTACT: San Joaquin Delta College, 5151 Pacific Avenue, Goleman 125, Stockton, CA 95207, (209) 474-5114.

[523] SAN JOAQUIN DELTA COLLEGE

ELIGIBILITY: The Minority Improvement Scholarship is awarded to a student who shows academic improvement and financial need. A 2.0 GPA is required.
AMOUNT: Varies
CONTACT: Financial Aid Director, San Joaquin Delta College, 5151 Pacific Avenue, Goleman 125, Stockton, CA 95207, (209) 474-5114.

[524] SCHOMBURG CENTER FOR RESEARCH IN BLACK CULTURE

ELIGIBILITY: Scholars-in-Residence Program. Open to scholars in the humanities studying black history and culture and to professionals in fields related to the Schomberg Center's collections and program activities. Fellows funded by the program will spend six months or one year in residence at the Schomberg Center. Deadline January 15.
AMOUNT: Varies
CONTACT: Scholars-in-Residence Program, Schomburg Center for Research in Black Culture, 515 Malcolm X Boulevard, New York, NY 10037-1801, (212) 491-2203.

[525] SCRIPPS HOWARD FOUNDATION SCHOLARSHIP

ELIGIBILITY: Students who are in good academic standing, demonstrate an interest in journalism and have financial need. Request an application during the month of November.
AMOUNT: $500 to $3,000
CONTACT: Scripps Howard Foundation Scholarship, P.O. Box 5380, Cincinnati, OH 45201.

[526] SHERMAN COLLEGE, SC

ELIGIBILITY: Minority Scholarship. The FAF is required. Student must submit an essay on why he or she chose a career in chiropractic medicine. Students may write to the financial aid office for information about other scholarships available to SCSC students. Financial need required. Deadline August 15.
AMOUNT: Varies
CONTACT: Financial Aid Officer, Sherman College, SC, P.O. Box 1452, Spartanburg, SC 29304, (803) 578-8770.

[527] SIERRA COMMUNITY COLLEGE

ELIGIBILITY: The Observer McDonald's Scholarship is awarded to black students who have completed 6 to 23 units and enroll full-time the following fall semester.
AMOUNT: $50

CONTACT: Sierra Community College, 5000 Rocklin Road, Rocklin, CA 95677, (916) 624-3333.

---

[528] SIGMA GAMMA RHO SORORITY NATIONAL EDUCATION FUND, INC.

ELIGIBILITY: The scholarship is available to students with a sincere interest in achieving a higher education. Applicants must be enrolled in or qualified for admission to an institution for higher education and must demonstrate need and scholastic ability.
AMOUNT: Varies
CONTACT: Dr. Jimmie C. Jackson, Scholarship Chairperson, 7135 8th Street, NW, Washington, DC 20012.

---

[529] SIMMONS COLLEGE

ELIGIBILITY: Dorothy Ferebee Scholarships. Offered to AHANA stduents who have distinguished themselves throughout high school.
AMOUNT: $3,000 a year for four years
CONTACT: Simmons College Admissions Office, Simmons College, 300 The Fenway, Boston, MA 02115, (617) 738-2107.

---

[530] SIOUX FALLS COLLEGE

ELIGIBILITY: Entering freshman must have a minimum ACT composite score of 19 or graduate in the upper half of their high school class. Limited funds are available to upperclass students with a 2.0 GPA. Deadline May 1.
AMOUNT: Varies
CONTACT: Director of Admissions, Sioux Falls College, 150 S. Prairie, Sioux Falls, SD 57105-1699, (605) 331-6600.

---

[531] SOCIETY OF ACTUARIES

ELIGIBILITY: Applicants must have taken the advanced mathematics test of the graduate record examination (GRE) or first actuarial exam. Deadline May 1.
AMOUNT: Varies

CONTACT: Scholarship Committee, Society of Actuaries, 500 Park Blvd., Itasca, IL 60143, (312) 773-3010.

[532] SOCIETY OF ACTUARIES
ELIGIBILITY: Minority Student Scholarships. Applicants must have taken the SAT or ACT test, have a 3.3 GPA, and be majoring in one of the following: insurance, actuarial science or mathematics. Deadline May 1.
AMOUNT: $2,500
CONTACT: Scholarship Committee, Society of Actuaries, 500 Park Blvd., Itasca, IL 60143, (313) 773-3010.

[533] SOUTHERN ILLINOIS UNIVERSITY
ELIGIBILITY: James M. & Aune P. Nelson Scholarship. Award to minority graduates of Alton Secondary Schools who have at least a 2.0 cumulative GPA in high school and a 2.5 GPA in college. Deadline March 1.
AMOUNT: Varies
CONTACT: Southern Illinois University, Attn: Office of Student Financial Aid, Rendleman Building, Box 1060, Edwardsville, IL 62026-1060, (618) 692-2562.

[534] SOUTHERN ILLINOIS UNIVERSITY AT EDWARDSVILLE
ELIGIBILITY: Minority Scholarship Program. Applicants must have a cumulative 3.5 (on a 5.0) GPA or equivalent, enroll in and satisfactorily complete 12 hours each quarter, and maintain a 3.5 GPA each quarter. Applicants must complete the ACT Family Financial Statement by April 1.
AMOUNT: Varies
CONTACT: Dr. Janet McReynolds, Assistant to the Provost and Vice President for Academic Affairs, Box 1021, SIUE, Edwardsville, IL 62026-1021, (618) 692-3778.

[535] UNIVERSITY OF SOUTH FLORIDA
ELIGIBILITY: The Richard Pride Research Fellowship is awarded to minority students persuing a Ph.D. at the University of South Florida in anthropology, biology, chemistry, English, marine science, mathematics, psychology, or communications. Applicants must be U.S. citizens. Deadline January 15.
AMOUNT: $15,000 + tuition
CONTACT: University of South Florida, Attn: Institute on Black Life, 4202 E. Fowler Avenue, SVC 1087, Tampa, FL 33260-6911, (813) 974-4727.

[536] SOUTHWESTERN UNIVERSITY
ELIGIBILITY: Presidential Scholar Award is for black and Hispanic students ranking in the top 10% of their high school class with at least a 3.5 GPA and 1150 SAT combined score or 25 ACT composite score.
AMOUNT: Tuition
CONTACT: Director of Admissions, Office of Admissions, Southwestern University, Georgetown, TX 78626, (512) 863-6511o r (800) 252-3166.

[537] SOUTHWESTERN UNIVERSITY SCHOOL OF LAW
ELIGIBILITY: Available to black students on the basis of community service, scholastic achievement, and financial need. Application forms are available in late November and selections are usually made in March. The money is available for the following academic year. Applicants must have successfully completed their first year of law school and have a 3.0 GPA. Recipients selected by wives of bench and bar. Deadline June 1.
AMOUNT: Varies
CONTACT: Southwestern University School of Law, 675 S. Westmoreland Avenue, Los Angeles, CA 90005, (213) 738-6719.

[538] SOUTHWESTERN UNIVERSITY SCHOOL OF LAW
ELIGIBILITY: The Tom Bradley Scholarship Fund is available to assist needy and deserving students. Must be in top 30% of their class. Not for entering students. Preference given to minority applicant in second or

third year of law school. Financial need required.
AMOUNT: $2,500
CONTACT: Financial Aid Director, Southwestern University School of Law, 675 S. Westmoreland Avenue, Los Angeles, CA 90005, (213) 738-6719.

[539] SPECIAL LIBRARIES ASSOCIATION
ELIGIBILITY: Minority Stipend Program. Applicants must be U.S. citizens or submit evidence of becoming naturalized at the beginning of the award period. Must be majoring in library science and financial need required. Deadline October 30.
AMOUNT: $3,000
CONTACT: Minority Groups Committee, Special Libraries Assn., 1700 Eighteenth Street, NW, Washington, DC 20009, (202) 234-4700.

[540] SPRING GARDEN COLLEGE
ELIGIBILITY: The President's Council Scholarship is awarded to an outstanding minority applicant on the basis of class rank and SAT scores. This award is renewable. Must be in the upper 1/5 of their class. Deadline March 1.
AMOUNT: Full tuition
CONTACT: Financial Aid Director, Spring Garden College, 7500 Germantown Avenue, Philadelphia, PA 19119, (215) 248-7905.

[541] STANLEY E. JACKSON SCHOLARSHIP FOR THE HANDICAPPED
ELIGIBILITY: Applicants must be handicapped and minority students who intend to enroll in full-time postsecondary education or training and are able to document financial need.
AMOUNT: $1,000
CONTACT: Foundation for Exceptional Children, 1920 Association Drive, Reston, VA 22091, (703) 630-3660.

[542] STATE STUDENT ASSISTANCE COMMISSION OF INDIANA

ELIGIBILITY: Minority Teacher Scholarship. Applicant must be a black U.S. citizen, have a 2.0 GPA, and major in education (special and pre-school included) Must teach three out of five years in Indiana following certification.

AMOUNT: $1,000

CONTACT: State Student Assistance Commission of Indiana, 964 N. Pennsylvania, 1st Floor, Indiana, IN 46208, (317) 251-1304.

[543] STILLMAN COLLEGE

ELIGIBILITY: Applicants must be black entering freshmen and have a strong academic background. Apply early.

AMOUNT: $100 to $2,000

CONTACT: Stillman College, P.O. Box Drawer 1430, Tuscaloosa, AL 35403 , (205) 349-4240 or (800) 841-5722.

[544] ST. JOHN FISHER COLLEGE

ELIGIBILITY: Minority Student Grants are available to the 10 best applicants. Must have a 3.0 GPA and financial need required.

AMOUNT: Half tuition

CONTACT: Director of Admissions, St. John Fisher College, 3690 East Avenue, Rochester, NY 14618, (716) 385-8064.

[545] ST. JOHN'S UNIVERSITY

ELIGIBILITY: Library Science Minority Fellowship. These grants are provided by the U.S. Department of Education. Contact the university for details.

AMOUNT: $4,000

CONTACT: Library Science Division, St. John's University, Grand Central & Utopia Parkway, Jamaica, NY 11439, (718) 990-6403.

[546] ST. MARY OF THE WOODS COLLEGE

ELIGIBILITY: Minority Leadership Award for a full-time female minority student who demonstrates leadership, community service, and commitment to achievement. Deadline August 15.
AMOUNT: $2,000
CONTACT: St. Mary of the Woods College, Attn: Director of Admissions/Financial Aid, Guerin Hall, St. Mary of the Woods, IN 47876, (812) 535-5106.

[547] ST. MARY'S COLLEGE OF MARYLAND

ELIGIBILITY: Offers several scholarship programs: Matthias D'Sousa Scholarships, General Scholarships, Brent Calvert Fellowship Honors Program, and The Waring Award. For example, the Matthias D'Sousa Scholarship is available to entering freshmen who are minority students and who are residents of Maryland. The award pays up to full tuition, room, and board, and is renewable. Deadline February 1.
AMOUNT: Varies
CONTACT: Office of Admissions, St. Mary's College of Maryland, St. Mary's City, MD 20686, (800) 492-7181.

[548] ST. PAUL'S COLLEGE

ELIGIBILITY: United Negro College Fund is available to entering black students. Must have a strong academic background. Apply early.
AMOUNT: $100 to $2,000
CONTACT: St. Paul's College, 406 Windsor Avenue, Lawrenceville, VA 23868, (804) 848-3111.

[549] ST. THOMAS CHURCH

ELIGIBILITY: The James Townsend Scholarship in Music. Applicant must be a black student enrolled as a freshman or sophomore in a college, university, or school of music. Selection is based on results of competitive auditions. Must be majoring in music or music vocals.
AMOUNT: $1,000
CONTACT: Mrs. Parthenia L. Twisdale, 11 Placid Lane, Willingboro, NJ 08046.

[550] STUDENT OPPORTUNITY SCHOLARSHIPS FOR ETHNIC MINORITY GROUPS

ELIGIBILITY: Minority students with financial need and recommended by counselors designated by the Church.
AMOUNT: $100 to $1,400
CONTACT: United Presbyterian Church in the U.S.A., 475 Riverside Drive, Rm. 430, New York, NY 10115, (212) 870-2618.

[551] SUNY-ONEONTA MINORITY HONORS SCHOLARSHIP

ELIGIBILITY: Student must be black, Hispanic, or American Indian. Must have a 3.0 GPA and financial need. Deadline May 1.
AMOUNT: Up to $1,000
CONTACT: Director of Financial Aid, State University of New York, Netzer Administration Bldg., Ravine Parkway, Oneonta, NY 13820, (607) 431-2532.

[552] SUNY-ONEONTA SCOTT-JENKINS MEMORIAL GRANT

ELIGIBILITY: Awarded to black or Hispanic students with a 2.0 GPA and who demonstrate financial need. Applicants must be U.S. citizens.
AMOUNT: $700
CONTACT: SUNY, Attn: Financial Aid Director, Netzer Administration Bldg., Ravine Parkway, Oneonta, NY 13820, (607) 431-2532.

[553] SYNOD OF THE TRINITY

ELIGIBILITY: Scholarships for minority students in several designated areas of the Presbytery surrounding Pennsylvania who must have been admitted to attend college and who demonstrate financial need.
AMOUNT: Varies
CONTACT: Synod of the Trinity, 3040 Market Street, Camp Hill, PA 17011.

[554] SYNOD OF THE TRINITY

ELIGIBILITY: Minority Scholarship Program. Applicants must live in West Virginia (does not include N.E. and S.W. counties in the panhandles). Applicants must demonstrate financial need, submit a narrative of career goals and family situation, file a transcript of grades, register with their financial aid office, and apply for federal (Pell) and state programs. Deadline March 1.
AMOUNT: $200 to $800
CONTACT: Minority Scholarship Program, 3040 Market Street, Camp Hill, PA 17011-4591, (717) 737-0421.

[555] SYRACUSE UNIVERSITY

ELIGIBILITY: WSYR Minority Award—open to candidates from an ethnic minority who wish to study broadcast journalism.
AMOUNT: $4,000
CONTACT: Office of Admissions, Syracuse University, Syracuse, NY 13210, (315) 423-1870.

[556] UNIVERSITY OF TENNESSEE

ELIGIBILITY: The Minority Engineering Scholarship Program (MESP) Awarded to African American high school students with a minimum GPA of 3.0, 23 on the ACT or 940 on the SAT, 3 1/2 units of math, and letters of recommendations from the following: counselor, math and science teachers. Deadline February.
AMOUNT: $11,000+
CONTACT: James T. Pippin, Assistant Dean, College of Engineering, University of Tennessee, 103 Estabrook Hall, Knoxville, TN 37996.

[557] TENNESSEE STATE UNIVERSITY

ELIGIBILITY: Must be black and have a 3.0 GPA. Deadline April 1.
AMOUNT: Tuition + room
CONTACT: Tennessee State University, 3500 John A. Merritt Blvd., Nashville, TN 37209-1561, (615) 320-3042.

[558] TENNESSEE STUDENT ASSISTANCE

ELIGIBILITY: Minority Teaching Fellowship. Must be a U.S. citizen with a 2.5 GPA, and be in the upper 2/5 of their class. 1 year teaching obligation per year of award. Forgivable loan program. Deadline May 15.
AMOUNT: $5,000
CONTACT: Program Administrator, Tennessee Student Assistance, Suite 1950, Parkway Towers, 404 James Robertson Parkway, Nashville, TN 37243, (615) 741-1346.

[559] TENNESSEE TECHNOLOGICAL UNIVERSITY

ELIGIBILITY: Minority Engineering Effort. Financial need required. Must be majoring in one of the following engineering areas: chemical, electrical, industrial, civil or mechanical.
AMOUNT: $250 to $2,500
CONTACT: Financial Aid Director, Tennessee Technological University, P.O. Box 5076, Cookeville, TN 38505, (615) 372-3888.

[560] TEXAS A & I UNIVERSITY

ELIGIBILITY: The National Action Council-ME Scholarship is open to new freshman, in the top 25% of their class who have a competitive ACT/SAT score, and who submit one letter of recommendation. The award is renewable with a 2.5 GPA. Deadline April 15.
AMOUNT: $1,000
CONTACT: Texas A & I University, Engineering Dept., Box 188, Kingsville, TX 78363, (512) 595-3907.

[561] TEXAS A & I UNIVERSITY

ELIGIBILITY: Atlantic Richfield Co. Scholarship. Applicant must have a competitive class rank and ACT/SAT score. The award is renewable with a 2.7 GPA. Must be majoring in chemical engineering or natural resources. Deadline November 15, April 1.
AMOUNT: $500
CONTACT: Dean, Chemical/Natural Gas, Texas A & I University, Chemical/Natural Gas, Box 193, Kingsville, TX 78363, (512) 595-3907.

[562] TEXAS A & I UNIVERSITY

ELIGIBILITY: Texas State Ethnic Recruitment. Available to non-Hispanic minorities who have financial need, who are in the top 33% of their class, and who have a 2.75 GPA. Applicants must also have a minimum ACT/SAT score of 18/800.
AMOUNT: $1,000
CONTACT: Financial Aid Director, Texas A & I University Financial Aid, Box 115, Kingsville, TX 78363, (512) 595-3907.

[563] TEXAS A & I UNIVERSITY

ELIGIBILITY: The 3M Foundation Scholarship. Applicants must have an ACT/SAT score of at least 22/950, and submit one letter of recommendation. The award is renewable with at least a 3.0 GPA. Must be a U.S. citizen, show financial need and be majoring in one of the following engineering areas: electrical, chemical, or mechanical.
AMOUNT: $1,000
CONTACT: Director of Admissions, Texas A & I University Engineering, Box 188, Kingsville, TX 78363, (512) 595-2111.

[564] TEXAS A & I UNIVERSITY

ELIGIBILITY: Larry and Charlotte Franklin Scholarship. Applicants must be active on the yearbook staff and majoring in journalism, be in the top 1/2 of their class, have a minimum ACT/SAT score of 18/800, a 2.75 GPA, and submit two letters of recommendation. Deadline May 1.
AMOUNT: $250
CONTACT: Dean, Communications Dept., Texas A & I University Communications, Box 178, Kingsville, TX 78363, (512) 595-3907.

[565] TEXAS A & M UNIVERSITY

ELIGIBILITY: Sponsors the President's Achievement Award for African-American and Hispanic students who are U.S. citizens or permanent residents admitted to the university. Stipends of $2,500 yearly for a total of $10,000 for four years of undergraduate study are awarded. On-campus housing is guaranteed to recipients submitting residence applications by June 1. Approximately 350 non-need based scholarship offers are made

annually. Applicants may compete for other Texas A&M scholarships including an additional $1,000 stipend for those participating in study abroad and awards to those seeking professional degrees at Texas A&M. Academic achievement, SAT or ACT test results and class rank are considered.
CONTACT: Texas A&M University, Office of School Relations, Memorial Student Center, College Station, TX 77843-1265, (409) 845-3741.

---

[566] TEXAS A & M UNIVERSITY
ELIGIBILITY: Minority Engineering Education. Financial need required. Must be majoring in agriculture or one of the following engineering areas: aerospace, biomedical, civil, industrial, nuclear, chemical, electrical, mechanical, petroleum. Deadline February 15.
AMOUNT: $500
CONTACT: Engineering Department, Texas A & M University, College Station, TX 77843-1252, (409) 845-7200.

---

[567] TEXAS A & M UNIVERSITY
ELIGIBILITY: The Minority Merit Fellowships are awarded to students who will begin graduate study toward a doctoral or master's degree in any field of study offered by the Texas A & M University at the College Station campus. Deadline March 1.
AMOUNT: $7,800
CONTACT: Admissions Office, Texas A & M University, College Station, TX 77843-1252, (409) 845-3631.

---

[568] TEXAS ALLIANCE FOR MINORITIES IN
ENGINEERING
ELIGIBILITY: The TAME program provides financial assistance and helps minority students gain admission.
AMOUNT: Varies
CONTACT: Texas Alliance for Minorities in Engineering, UTA Station 19775, Arlington, TX 76019.

---

[569] TEXAS BLACK BAPTIST SCHOLARSHIP

ELIGIBILITY: Awarded to resident of Texas attending a Texas school with a minimum GPA of 2.0 (3.0 if a high school senior) and who possesses a vital interest in the advancement of the Kingdom of God.
AMOUNT: $800 a year
CONTACT: Texas Black Baptist Scholarship Committee, Black Church Relations Section, Attn: James W. Culp, Sr., 333 North Washington, Suite 371, Dallas, TX 74246-1798, (214) 828-5100.

[570] TEXAS STATE SCHOLARSHIP PROGRAM FOR ETHNIC RECRUITMENT

ELIGIBILITY: Students whose ethnic group comprises less than 40% of the enrollment at a particular institution may be eligible for a scholarship. Entering freshmen must attain an ACT score of at least 18, and transfer students must have at least a 2.75 GPA.
AMOUNT: $500 to $1,000
CONTACT: Texas Higher Education Coordinating Board, P.O. Box 12788, Capitol Station, Austin, TX 78711, (512) 483-6340.

[571] UNIVERSITY OF TEXAS, ARLINGTON

ELIGIBILITY: Ethnic Recruitment Scholarship. Applicants must be residents of Texas. Entering freshman must rank in the upper 1/3 of their high school graduating class or have a minimum SAT combined score of 800 or a minimum ACT composite score of 18. Entering transfer students must have a grade average of at least 2.75 at the college they last attended.
AMOUNT: $500
CONTACT: Scholarship Office, University of Texas, Box 19199, Arlington, TX 76019, (817) 273-2197.

[572] UNIVERSITY OF TEXAS AT AUSTIN

ELIGIBILITY: Accounting Scholarships are available to minority students majoring in accounting.
AMOUNT: Varies
CONTACT: Office of Admissions, University of Texas at Austin, Austin, TX 78712, (512) 471-3434.

[573] UNIVERSITY OF TEXAS AT AUSTIN

ELIGIBILITY: Minority Business Assistance—for students in the College of Business Administration.
AMOUNT: Varies
CONTACT: Office of Admissions, University of Texas at Austin, Austin, TX 78712, (512) 471-3434.

[574] UNIVERSITY OF TEXAS AT AUSTIN

ELIGIBILITY: Texas Achievement Awards—designed for selected minority freshman who show academic potential.
AMOUNT: $1,000
CONTACT: Office of Admissions, University of Texas at Austin, Austin, TX 78712, (512) 471-3434.

[575] UNIVERSITY OF TEXAS AT EL PASO

ELIGIBILITY: The Minority Engineering Award. Must show financial need and be majoring in one of the following engineering fields: civil, metallurgy, electrical and mechanical.
AMOUNT: $250 to $1,000
CONTACT: University of Texas at El Paso, 500 W. University Avenue, El Paso, TX 79968, (915) 747-5204.

[576] TEXAS SOUTHERN UNIVERSITY

ELIGIBILITY: The Julius A. Thomas Fellowship program was created to offer minority individuals an opportunity for master's level education in a field to enable them to serve the career counseling and placement needs of minority and disadvantaged students. In addition, an allowance of up to $150 for approved books and materials is available. Persons interested should apply for the program at one of the six participating institutions and indicate an interest in the Thomas Fellowship Program. Contact the Dean for instructional services at Texas Southern University for additional information. Deadline May 1.
AMOUNT: $3,000
CONTACT: College Placement Services, 62 Highland Avenue, Bethlehem, PA 18017, (215) 868-2523.

[577] THOMAS A. WATSON SCHOLARSHIP

ELIGIBILITY: Applicant must be a minority student from an Allen County high school. Scholarships must be used at an approved and accredited school in Indiana or a state bordering Indiana (Kentucky, Illinois, Michigan, or Ohio) Must be majoring in one of the following: business administration/management, mathematics, insurance, accounting, computer science/data processing, finance, or actuarial science.
CONTACT: Scholarship Chairman, Lincoln National Life Insurance, 1300 S. Clinton Street, P.O. Box 1110, Fort Wayne, IN 46801.

[578] THURGOOD MARSHALL SCHOLARSHIP FUND

ELIGIBILITY: Available for students at historically black public colleges or universities with a 3.0 GPA, an ACT score of at least 24, or a SAT combined score of 1000. Deadline May 1.
AMOUNT: $16,000 over a four year period
CONTACT: The Thurgood Marshall Scholarship Fund, 100 Park Avenue, 10th Floor, New York, NY 10017.

[579] THE TILLIE GOLUB-SCHWARTZ MEMORIAL SCHOLARSHIP

ELIGIBILITY: Must be a minority and show a commitment to humanity.
AMOUNT: $8,000 (4 years)
CONTACT: Scholarship Committee, Golub Corporation, P.O. Box 1074, Schenectady, NY 12301.

[580] UNIVERSITY OF TOLEDO MINORITY SCHOLARSHIP

ELIGIBILITY: Applicants must be U.S. citizens, majoring in engineering and have a 3.0 GPA.
AMOUNT: $1,000
CONTACT: Office of Admissions, University of Toledo, 2801 W. Bancroft, Toledo, OH 43606, (419) 537-2696.

[581] TOWSON STATE UNIVERSITY

ELIGIBILITY: Towson State gives at least 15 Minority Awards for Academic Excellence to full-time freshman and transfer students. Academic achievement and leadership potential are criteria. Applicants must be Maryland residents with a 2.75+ GPA and a 1000 combined SAT score. Transfers must be Maryland residents with a 2.75 GPA and an AA degree from a Maryland community college. Deadline January 1.
AMOUNT: $1,000 to full tuition and fees
CONTACT: Admissions Office, Towson State University, Administration Bldg., Room 324, Towson, MD 21204-7097, (410) 830-2113.

[582] TRINITY UNIVERSITY

ELIGIBILITY: Minority Scholarships are awarded to those recognized through National Achievement or National Hispanic Scholarship programs.
AMOUNT: $1,000 to $4,000
CONTACT: Director, Trinity University, Minority Scholarships Financial Aid Office, 715 Stadium Drive, San Antonio, TX 78284, (512) 736-8315.

[583] TUSKEGEE UNIVERSITY

ELIGIBILITY: The United Negro College Fund is awarded to a black entering freshman. Must have a strong academic background. Apply early.
AMOUNT: $1,000 - $2,000
CONTACT: Office of Financial Aid, Tuskegee University, Tuskegee, AL 36088, (212) 867-1100.

[584] UNION COLLEGE

ELIGIBILITY: The Chester Arthur Undergraduate Support of Excellence Awards (CAUSE) offers financial aid in the form of cancelable loans for students engaging in public service-oriented activities.
AMOUNT: Varies
CONTACT: Admissions Office, Becker Hall, Union College, Schenectady, NY 12308, (518) 370-6131.

[585] UNION COLLEGE

ELIGIBILITY: IBM Scholarship Fund is available to women and minority engineering students. Financial need required.
AMOUNT: Varies
CONTACT: Union College, Stanley R. Becker Hall, Schenectady, NY 12308.

[586] UNITED CHURCH OF CHRIST COMMISSION FOR RACIAL JUSTICE; SPECIAL HIGHER EDUCATION PROGRAM

ELIGIBILITY: Offers supplemental scholarships to needy students; awards given each semester.
AMOUNT: Varies
CONTACT: United Church of Christ Commission for Racial Justice Special Higher Education Program, 105 Madison Avenue, New York, NY 10016, (212) 533-7370.

[587] UNITED CHURCH OF CHRIST, SOUTHERN CALIFORNIA

ELIGIBILITY: Seaman Scholarship awarded to a female student. Deadline May 6.
AMOUNT: Varies
CONTACT: United Church of Christ, Southern California Conference, c/o Women in Mission Commission, Attn: Josephine Seaman Scholarship Committee, 466 E. Walnut Street, Pasadena, CA 91101-1690, (818) 449-6026.

[588] UNITED METHODIST CHURCH

ELIGIBILITY: Crusade Scholarship Program. Must show promise of providing leadership for the church and society. Deadline February 1.
AMOUNT: Varies
CONTACT: Mission Personnel Resources Program Dept., General Board of Global Ministers, Suite 1470, 475 Riverside Drive, New York, NY 10115.

[589] UNITED METHODIST CHURCH

ELIGIBILITY: HANA Scholars Program awards ethnic scholarships to minority United Methodist Church members with financial need for undergraduate studies.
AMOUNT: Up to $1,000
CONTACT: United Methodist Church, Board of Higher Education and Ministry, P.O. Box 871, Nashville, TN 37202, (615) 327-2700.

[590] UNITED METHODIST CHURCH ETHNIC MINORITY SCHOLARSHIPS

ELIGIBILITY: Minority students who are active in the United Methodist Church, recommended by their pastor, enrolled in an accredited college, and in financial need.
AMOUNT: $100 to $1,000
CONTACT: United Methodist Church Board of Higher Education and Ministry, P.O. Box 871, Nashville, TN 37202, (615) 327-2700.

[591] UNITED METHODIST COMMUNICATION

ELIGIBILITY: Leonard M. Perryman Communication Scholarship. Awarded to minority students persuing a career in religious communications. Deadline February 1.
AMOUNT: $2,500
CONTACT: Nelson Price, United Methodist Communication, Suite 1901, 475 Riverside Drive, New York, NY 10115.

[592] UNITED METHODIST PUBLISHING HOUSE MERIT SCHOLARSHIP PROGRAM

ELIGIBILITY: For those interested in employment with United Methodist Church or United Methodist Publishing House. Deadline March 15.
AMOUNT: Varies
CONTACT: Office of Loans & Scholarships, The United Methodist Church Merit Scholarship Program, P.O. Box 871, Nashville, TN 37202-0871, (615) 327-2700.

[593] UNITED NEGRO COLLEGE FUND
SCHOLARSHIPS

ELIGIBILITY: Qualified applicants are considered without regard to race, creed, color, or national origin. Individual member colleges where students have applied for admission select scholarship recipients. Applications and selection of recipients are not administered by the United Negro College Fund. Students must take the SAT test (Dec. exam). The United Negro College Fund administers full support MBA fellowships. Applicants must have a 3.0 GPA, majoring in engineering, and have financial need. Write for details.
AMOUNT: $1,000 to $2,000
CONTACT: United Negro Scholarship Fund, 500 E. 62nd Street, New York, NY 10021, (212) 644-9712.

[594] THE UNITED NEGRO SCHOLARSHIP FUND

ELIGIBILITY: General Motors Engineering Scholarship. Students must be enrolled in a UNCF college or university, must demonstrate need, and must have a 2.5 GPA. Inquiries must be made to the financial aid office at each school.
AMOUNT: Varies
CONTACT: General Motors Engineering Scholarship, UNCF, 8260 Willow Oaks Corporate Drive, P.O. Box 10444, Fairfax, VA 22031-4511.

[595] THE UNITED NEGRO SCHOLARSHIP FUND

ELIGIBILITY: Janet Jackson Rhythm Nation Scholarship for performing arts. Students must be enrolled in a UNCF college or university, must demonstrate need, and must have a a 2.5 GPA. Inquiries must be made to the financial aid office at each school.
AMOUNT: Varies
CONTACT: Janet Jackson Rhythm Nation Scholarship, UNCF, 8260 Willow Oaks Corporate Drive, P.O. Box 10444, Fairfax, VA 22031-4511.

[596] THE UNITED NEGRO SCHOLARSHIP FUND

ELIGIBILITY: Michael Jackson Scholarship for performing arts. Students must be enrolled in a UNCF college or university, must demonstrate need, and must have a a 2.5 GPA. Inquiries must be made to the financial aid office at each school.
AMOUNT: Varies
CONTACT: Michael Jackson Scholarship, UNCF, 8260 Willow Oaks Corporate Drive, P.O. Box 10444, Fairfax, VA 22031-4511.

[597] THE UNITED NEGRO SCHOLARSHIP FUND

ELIGIBILITY: Stan Scott Endowed Scholarship for journalism. Students must be enrolled in a UNCF college or university, must demonstrate need, and must have a a 2.5 GPA. Inquiries must be made to the financial aid office at each school.
AMOUNT: Varies
CONTACT: Stan Scott Endowed Scholarship, UNCF, 8260 Willow Oaks Corporate Drive, P.O. Box 10444, Fairfax, VA 22031-4511.

[598] THE UNITED PRESBYTERIAN CHURCH IN THE U.S.A.

ELIGIBILITY: National Presbyterian College Scholarships. Awarded to superior young people preparing to enter as freshmen at one of the participating colleges related to the United Presbyterian Church in the U.S.A. Students must be a communicant member of the United Presbyterian Church and must demonstrate financial need. Deadline December 1.
AMOUNT: $100 to $1,400
CONTACT: The United Presbyterian Church in the U.S.A., 475 Riverside Drive, Room 430, New York, NY 10027, (212) 870-2618.

[599] THE UNITED PRESBYTERIAN CHURCH IN THE U.S.A.

ELIGIBILITY: Student Opportunity Scholarships. For young persons of limited opportunities who are of ethnic minority groups and are related to the United Presbyterian Church in the U.S.A. Students must be a U.S.

citizen, must be entering as a freshman, must be a full-time student, and must apply to the college for financial aid.
AMOUNT: $100 to $1,400
CONTACT: The United Presbyterian Church in the U.S.A., 475 Riverside Drive, Room 430, New York, NY 10027, (212) 870-2618.

---

[600] UTAH STATE UNIVERSITY

ELIGIBILITY: Minority Engineering Scholarship For those majoring in one of the following engineering areas: civil, metallurgy, electrical, mechanical or agriculture. Financial need required. Deadline is September 1.
AMOUNT: $250 to $2,500
CONTACT: Utah State University, Logan, UT 84322-7700, (801) 797-1000.

---

[601] VALPARAISO UNIVERSITY

ELIGIBILITY: The Henry L. Prahl Scholarship Fund is available to a minority student majoring in education.
AMOUNT: Varies
CONTACT: Financial Aid Director, Valparaiso University, Valparaiso, IN 46383, (219) 464-5000.

---

[602] VILLANOVA UNIVERSITY

ELIGIBILITY: Scholarships for black Americans are for students who wish to attend Villanova University as commuters. Applicants must be a U.S. citizen and in the upper 1/5 of their class.
AMOUNT: Tuition
CONTACT: Villanova University, Minority Recruiter, Villanova, PA 19085-1672, (215) 645-4004.

---

[603] VIRGINIA COMMONWEALTH UNIVERSITY

ELIGIBILITY: The Coca-Cola Scholarship is awarded to entering black students who are U.S. citizens. Applicants must have a 3.5 GPA, be in the upper 1/5 of their class, and major in accounting, art, marketing, or

business administration/management. SAT score—1,000; ACT score—
23. Deadline March 1.
AMOUNT: $2,415
CONTACT: UES/Office of Admissions, Virginia Commonwealth Univ.,
821 W. Franklin Street, Box 2526, Richmond, VA 23284, (804) 367-
1222.

[604] VIRGINIA COMMONWEALTH UNIVERSITY
ELIGIBILITY: The Black Freshman Scholarship Program is for enter-
ing freshman with a GPA of 3.0. Applicants must be U.S. citizens and in
the upper 1/5 of their class. Deadline March 1.
AMOUNT: $1,000 to $1,200
CONTACT: UES/Admissions, Virginia Commonwealth Univ., 821 W.
Franklin Street, Box 2526, Richmond, VA 23284, (804) 367-1222.

[605] VIRGINIA UNION UNIVERSITY
ELIGIBILITY: The United Negro College Fund is for black freshman.
Must have a strong academic background. Apply early.
AMOUNT: $100 to $2,000
CONTACT: Virginia Union University, 1500 N. Lombardy Street,
Richmond, VA 23220, (804) 257-5881 or (800) 368-3227.

[606] UNIVERSITY OF VIRGINIA
ELIGIBILITY: J. H. Holland Scholarship is awarded to black students
who are U.S. citizens. Applicants must reside outside the state of VA.
Deadline January 15.
AMOUNT: $5,000
CONTACT: Director of Financial Aid, University of Virginia, P.O. Box
9021, Miller Hall, Charlottesville, VA 22906, (804) 924-3725.

[607] UNIVERSITY OF VIRGINIA
ELIGIBILITY: The University Achievement Award is for exceptional
black students in the state of Virginia and is renewable with satisfactory
academic progress.

AMOUNT: Tuition
CONTACT: University of Virginia—Charlottesville, Office of Financial Aid, P.O. Box 9021, Miller Hall, Charlottesville, VA 22906, (804) 924-3725.

---

[608] UNIVERSITY OF VIRGINIA
ELIGIBILITY: Financial need required. Must be majoring in one of the following engineering areas: aerospace, civil, mechanical, chemical or electrical.
AMOUNT: $250 to $2,500
CONTACT: Financial Aid Director, University of Virginia, P.O. Box 9021, Miller Hall, Charlottesville, VA 22906, (804) 924-3725.

---

[609] VOORHEES COLLEGE
ELIGIBILITY: The United Negro College Fund is for entering freshman. Must have a strong academic background. Apply early.
AMOUNT: $100 to $2,000
CONTACT: Voorhees College, Voorhees Road, Denmark, SC 29042.

---

[610] W. W. SMITH FOUNDATION
ELIGIBILITY: Awards for students attending Cheyney University.
AMOUNT: $2,000 renewable
CONTACT: James Brown, Cheyney University of Pennsylvania, Cheyney, PA 19319, (215) 399-2302.

---

[611] WARREN WILSON COLLEGE
ELIGIBILITY: Students must rank in the top 20 percent of their class and must submit an essay and letters of recommendation.
AMOUNT: $1,500
CONTACT: Warren Wilson College, Admissions Office, 701 Warren Wilson College Road, Swannanoa, NC 28778, (704) 298-3325.

---

[612] WASHINGTON STATE NEED GRANT
ELIGIBILITY: Student must be needy or disadvantaged, a Washington resident, and enrolled or accepted as a full-time undergraduate student.
AMOUNT: $300 to $570
CONTACT: Washington Council for Postsecondary Education, 908 E. Fifth Street, Olympia, WA 98504, (206) 753-3571.

[613] WASHINGTON UNIVERSITY
ELIGIBILITY: John B. Ervin Scholarship Competition for Black Americans. Awarded to high school seniors who apply and are admitted as freshmen to Washington University. Deadline January 15.
AMOUNT: Tuition plus stipend
CONTACT: John B. Ervin Scholarship Competition, Washington University, Campus Box 1089, One Brookings Drive, St. Louis, MO 63130, (800) 638-0700.

[614] WASHINGTON URBAN LEAGUE GRANDMET/ NATIONAL URBAN LEAGUE, ESSAY CONTEST
ELIGIBILITY: Participants must be entering college freshmen or undergraduate college students who will be attending an accredited institution of higher learning. Awards will be made payable to the institution. Essays must be between 500 and 1,000 words and be typewritten and double spaced or legibly handwritten and must include participant's full name and permanent address. Entries will be judged for content, originality, organization, style, grammar, spelling, punctuation, and neatness. Contact your high school guidance counselor or college counselor for additional information and this year's topic and deadline.
AMOUNT: $1,000
CONTACT: Deputy Director, Northern Virginia Branch, Washington Urban League, Inc., 901 N. Washington Street, #202, Alexandria, VA 22314, (703) 836-2858.

[615] WEST CHESTER UNIVERSITY
ELIGIBILITY: Minority Academically Talented Award. Evaluation includes successful completion of an academic high school program,

successful high school class rank, satisfactory SAT or ACT scores, an essay discussing contribution to the school/community, and 3 letters of recommendation. Deadline March 1.
AMOUNT: Varies
CONTACT: Director of Admissions, West Chester University Office of Admissions, 110 Rosedale Avenue, West Chester, PA 19383, (610) 436-2627.

[616] UNIVERSITY OF WEST FLORIDA
ELIGIBILITY: Equal Education Opportunity Grant. Renewable with a 2.3 GPA for undergraduates and 3.2 for graduate students.
AMOUNT: $500
CONTACT: Financial Aid Director, The University of West Florida, 11000 University Pkwy., Pensacola, FL 32514, (904) 474-2400.

[617] WEST GEORGIA COLLEGE
ELIGIBILITY: These minority scholarships are awarded to black students who have demonstrated outstanding academic achievement. Entering freshman will receive a total of $3,000 over four years. Deadline March 1.
AMOUNT: $750 per year
CONTACT: Director of Admissions, West Georgia College, Carrollton, GA 30118, (404) 836-6416.

[618] WEST VIRGINIA STATE COLLEGE
ELIGIBILITY: Marguerite Thornton Scholarship awarded to a full-time black student with a 2.0 GPA. Applicant must be a resident of Pennsylvania and show financial need. Three letters of recommendation required. Deadline April 22.
AMOUNT: Varies
CONTACT: Marguerite Brower Thornton Family, Attn: Marguerite Thornton Scholarship, 1517 W. Pike Street, Philadelphia, PA 19140, (215) 225-4462.

[619] WESTERN MICHIGAN UNIVERSITY

ELIGIBILITY: The Alfred Griffin Scholarship Fund is to support a senior in early elementary education. Covers 1/2 of the recipient's tuition each semester; black or Native American preferred. Must have a 2.5 GPA.
AMOUNT: 1/2 tuition
CONTACT: Western Michigan University, College of Education, 2306 Sangren Hall, Kalamazoo, MI 49008-3899, (616) 387-3465.

[620] WESTERN MICHIGAN UNIVERSITY

ELIGIBILITY: Approximately 55 predoctoral fellowships and 20 dissertation fellowships for designated minorities to be awarded in a nationwide competition sponsored by the Ford Foundation and administered by the National Research Council. Each predoctoral award includes an annual stipend of $11,000 to the fellow; each predoctoral award provides up to a maximum of three years of support. Each dissertation award consists of an annual stipend of $18,000 to the fellow; dissertation awards are not renewable. There will be no dependency or travel allowances for predoctoral and dissertation fellows. Must be a U.S. citizen and be majoring in social science, engineering, science, humanities or mathematics.
AMOUNT: $10,350 to $18,000
CONTACT: Western Michigan University, Office of Financial Aid, Kalamazoo, MI 49008-3899, (616) 383-1806.

[621] WESTERN MICHIGAN UNIVERSITY

ELIGIBILITY: The Thurgood Marshall Assistantships. Students from minority groups admitted to degree program with demonstrated scholarship and financial need and who participate in the professional activities of the department are eligible.
AMOUNT: $6,900/3 semesters
CONTACT: Marshall Assistantships Administration, Western Michigan University, The Graduate College, Kalamazoo, MI 49008, (616) 383-1806.

[622] WESTERN MICHIGAN UNIVERSITY
ELIGIBILITY: Whitney Young Scholar's Program. Applicants must be either seniors or first year graduate students, and must have demonstrated excellence in scholarship and community service. Applicants are recommended by university personnel and must major in social work.
AMOUNT: Varies
CONTACT: Western Michigan University, School of Social Work, College of Health & Human Services, Kalamazoo, MI 49008-3899, (616) 387-3180.

[623] WESTERN MICHIGAN UNIVERSITY
ELIGIBILITY: The Ann C. Mountjoy Memorial Scholarship is awarded to an outstanding, minority, undergraduate psychology major.
CONTACT: Dept. Chairman, Western Michigan University, Dept. of Psychology, Kalamazoo, MI 49008-3899, (616) 387-4498.

[624] WESTERN MICHIGAN UNIVERSITY
ELIGIBILITY: Martin L. King, Jr.—Cesar Chavez—Rosa Parks. For minority undergraduates declaring education as their area of study.
AMOUNT: $1,500
CONTACT: Education Dean's Office, Western Michigan University, College of Education, 2306 Sangren Hall, Kalamazoo, MI 49008-3899, (616) 387-3465.

[625] WESTERN MICHIGAN UNIVERSITY
ELIGIBILITY: Higher Education Incentive Scholarship—Minorities. This renewable award is based on academic excellence and a competition. Extracurricular activities are considered. A 3.5 GPA computed by Western Michigan is a requirement.
AMOUNT: $3,000
CONTACT: Incentive Scholarship Officer, Western Michigan University, WMU Minority Student Services, Kalamazoo, MI 49008, (616) 383-1806.

[626] WESTERN WASHINGTON UNIVERSITY

ELIGIBILITY: The Martin Luther King, Jr., Scholarship is awarded to a black American returning to Western. Selection is based on leadership ability, academic achievement, community activities, and club participation. Applicant must be in the upper 1/5 of the class. Deadline April 15.
AMOUNT: Varies
CONTACT: Multi-Cultural Center, 516 High Street, Western Washington University, Bellingham, WA 98225, (206) 676-3843.

[627] WESTERN WASHINGTON UNIVERSITY

ELIGIBILITY: Minority Achievement Program Scholarships. Applicants may be freshman or transfer students with strong academic promise. A faculty mentor program matches students with faculty of the student's academic interest. Deadline April 15.
AMOUNT: $1,000
CONTACT: Multi-Cultural Center, 516 High Street, Western Washington University, Bellingham, WA 98225, (206) 676-3843.

[628] WESTERN WASHINGTON UNIVERSITY

ELIGIBILITY: Ford Foundation Postdoctoral Fellowships for Minorities. In this national competition sponsored by the Ford Foundation, citizens of the U.S. who are members of one of the designated minority groups, who are preparing for or already engaged in college or university teaching, and who have held the Ph.D. or Sc.D. degree for less than 7 years may apply for a fellowship award of one year's duration. Must be majoring on one of the following: science, humanities, physical science, engineering, social science, or mathematics. Deadline January 12.
AMOUNT: $25,000
CONTACT: Multi-Cultural Center, 516 High Street, Western Washington University, Bellingham, WA 98225, (206) 676-3843.

[629] WICHITA STATE UNIVERSITY

ELIGIBILITY: The Minority Engineering Scholarship is awarded to a minority majoring in one of the following engineering fields: electrical, mechanical, aerospace or geological. Deadline September 1.

AMOUNT: Varies
CONTACT: Wichita State University, Campus Box 24, 1845 N. Fairmount, Wichita, KS 67208-1595, (316) 689-3430.

[630] WILBERFORCE UNIVERSITY
ELIGIBILITY: The United Negro College Fund is awarded to black Wilberforce students. Must have a strong academic background. Apply early.
AMOUNT: $100 to $2,000
CONTACT: Wilberforce University, Wilberforce, OH 45384, (513) 376-2911.

[631] WILLIAMS COLLEGE
ELIGIBILITY: Gaius Charles Bolin Fellowships for Minority Graduate Students interested in pursuing careers in college teaching. The fellowship gives a minority graduate student time to complete dissertation work while working toward the Ph.D. in the humanities or in the natural, social or behavioral sciences. Additionally, fellows teach a one-semester course and are assigned a faculty advisor during the year of residence.
CONTACT: John Reichert, Dean of the Faculty, Hopkins Hall, Williams College, Williamstown, MA 01267, (413) 597-4351.

[632] WILMINGTON COLLEGE
ELIGIBILITY: Minority Leader Scholarship Must be involved in leadership capacity in extracurricular activity. Rank in upper 3/5. Must have a 2.5 GPA. Deadline November 15, January 15.
AMOUNT: $3,000
CONTACT: Office of Admissions, Wilmington College, Pyle Center, Box 1325, Wilmington, OH 45177, (513) 382-1661.

[633] UNIVERSITY OF WISCONSIN AT MADISON
ELIGIBILITY: The Grant Foundation Scholarship program makes several awards for minority students studying journalism.
AMOUNT: $800

CONTACT: Office of Admissions, University of Wisconsin at Madison, 500 Lincoln Drive, Madison, WI 53706, (608) 262-1234.

[634] UNIVERSITY OF WISCONSIN AT OSHKOSH
ELIGIBILITY: Minority Honor Scholarship. Awarded to a minority student in the top 25 percent of their class. Must be a U.S. citizen or have permanent residency. Deadline February 15.
AMOUNT: $500 to $2,000
CONTACT: University of Wisconsin, Attn: Director of Admissions, 800 Algoma Boulevard, Oshkosh, WI 54901, (414) 424-0202.

[635] UNIVERSITY OF WISCONSIN, PLATTEVILLE
ELIGIBILITY: The Engineering Development Scholarship is available for entering minority women majoring in one of the following engineering fields: civil, industrial, electrical or mechanical.
AMOUNT: $200
CONTACT: University of Wisconsin, Platteville Campus, 1 University Plaza, Platteville, WI 53818, (608) 342-1125.

[636] WISCONSIN MINORITY STUDENT GRANT
PROGRAM
ELIGIBILITY: Black students enrolled in private, non-profit institutions of higher education in Wisconsin may apply.
AMOUNT: Varies
CONTACT: Higher Education Aids Board, P.O. Box 7885, Madison, WI 53707-7885, (608) 267-2206.

[637] THE WOODROW WILSON NATIONAL
FELLOWSHIP FOUNDATION
ELIGIBILITY: Awards for minority students who have completed their junior year in college and who are interested in government careers. Students must attend an accredited summer institute.
AMOUNT: $6,000
CONTACT: Judith Pinch, Vice President, The Woodrow Wilson Na-

tional Fellowship Foundation, 330 Alexander Street, Box 642, Princeton, NJ 08542, (609) 924-4666.

---

[638] WORLD INSTITUTE OF BLACK COMMUNICATIONS, INC.

ELIGIBILITY: Four A's African American Student Scholarships awarded to black American men and women interested in advertising. Students must have been participants in the American Association of Advertising Agencies' Minority Advertising Intern Program.
AMOUNT: $1,000 to $2,000
CONTACT: World Institute of Black Communications, Inc., 10 Columbus Circle, New York, NY 10019, (212) 586-1771.

---

[639] WRIGHT STATE UNIVERSITY

ELIGIBILITY: Paul Laurence Dunbar Scholarships to African-American students who score a composite 20 ACT or 870 SAT, complete a college prep curriculum, and rank in top 20 percent at the end of seventh semester or have a 3.0 GPA. Deadline is March 31 for application and Financial Aid Form.
AMOUNT: $2,000
CONTACT: Coordinator of Scholarships, Office of Financial Aid, Wright State University, Dayton, OH 45401, (513) 873-2321.

---

[640] XAVIER UNIVERSITY

ELIGIBILITY: Xavier Academic Award given to a student with a math SAT score of at least 400, a verbal SAT score of at least 400, and an ACT score of at least 20. Student must be ranked in the top 20 percent of his or her class. Deadine April 15.
AMOUNT: $2,500
CONTACT: Xavier University, Attn: Director of Admissions, 3800 Victory Parkway, Cincinnati, OH 45207-5311, (513) 745-3301.

[641] XAVIER UNIVERSITY

ELIGIBILITY: Fr. Pedro Arrupe, S. J. Scholarship. Awarded every four years and will be awarded again in the fall of 1996. For African-American students.
AMOUNT: Tuition
CONTACT: Xavier University, Attn: Director of Admissions, 3800 Victory Parkway, Cincinnati, OH 45207-5311, (513) 745-3301.

[642] XAVIER UNIVERSITY

ELIGIBILITY: United Negro College Fund is awarded to black college freshman. Must have a strong academic background. Apply early.
AMOUNT: $100 to $2,000
CONTACT: Xavier University, 7325 Palmetto Street, New Orleans, LA 70125, (504) 486-7411.

[643] XEROX CORPORATION

ELIGIBILITY: Scholarships to minority students studying engineering or science.
AMOUNT: Up to $4,000 a year
CONTACT: Xerox Corporation, P.O. Box 1600, Stamford, CT 06904.

[644] XEROX TECHNICAL SCHOLARSHIPS

ELIGIBILITY: Awards to minority students enrolled full-time in science or engineering college programs. Deadline August 1.
AMOUNT: Varies
CONTACT: Xerox Technical Scholarships, College Relations, Xerox Corporation, Building 205LL, 800 Phillips Road, Webster, NY 14580.

[645] YMCA KATE H. ATHERTON SCHOLARSHIP

ELIGIBILITY: Grants are available only to female residents of the state of Hawaii (preferably minorities), who are pursuing a college education in Hawaii or in the continental United States.
AMOUNT: Up to $1,500
CONTACT: Hawaiian Trust Company, Ltd., P.O. Box 3170, Honolulu, HI 96802, (808) 525-8511.

[646] ZETA DELTA PHI SORORITY

ELIGIBILITY: This sorority promotes academic excellence and offers scholarships to qualified black high school students.
AMOUNT: Varies
CONTACT: Zeta Delta Phi Sorority, Inc., P.O. Box 157, Bronx, NY 10469, (212) 407-8288.

[647] ZETA PHI BETA SORORITY

ELIGIBILITY: The Deborah P. Wolfe International Fellowship is awarded to black women for a full academic year for full-time study in the U.S. for a foreign student. Deadline February 1.
AMOUNT: Varies
CONTACT: Zeta Phi Beta Sorority, 1201 Boynton Avenue, Westfield, NJ 07090.

[648] ZETA PHI BETA SORORITY

ELIGIBILITY: The Nancy B. Woolridge Graduate Fellowship is awarded to Zeta Phi Beta members in good standing. Must show good character, exemplify high ideals, and be active in the sorority. Applicants must write a 10-page essay on why the scholarship request is being made. Applicants must have at least a 2.0 GPA. Write for details.
AMOUNT: Varies
CONTACT: Zeta Phi Beta Sorority, Inc., 1734 New Hampshire Avenue, NW, Washington, DC 20009, (202) 387-3103.

[649] ZETA PHI BETA SORORITY

ELIGIBILITY: African Fellowship is awarded to an active black member of Zeta Phi Beta Sorority. Official application form should be secured from national headquarters of Zeta Phi Beta Sorority or directly from the chairperson of the scholarship committee. Applicant must supply proof of matriculation. Deadline: February 1.
AMOUNT: Not to exceed $1,000
CONTACT: Zeta Phi Beta Sorority, c/o Brenda K. Green, 1514 North 25th Street, Baton Rouge, LA 70802.

[650] ZETA PHI BETA SORORITY

ELIGIBILITY: The Mildred C. Bradham Social Work Fellowship. Applicants must be of good character, have an outstanding academic record, demonstrate leadership ability, and be recommended by a graduate chapter of Zeta Phi Beta Sorority. Applicants must write a 10-page essay on why the scholarship request is being made. Award is renewable. Write for details. Deadline March 1.

AMOUNT: Varies

CONTACT: Zeta Phi Beta Sorority, 1734 New Hampshire Avenue, NW, Washington, DC 20009, (202) 387-3103.

---

[651] ZETA PHI BETA SORORITY

ELIGIBILITY: The National Education Foundation. Applicants may or may not be members of Zeta Phi Beta. This is for graduate women who are working on a professional degree, masters, doctorate, or post-doctoral study.

AMOUNT: Up to $2,500

CONTACT: Zeta Phi Beta Sorority, 1827 79th Avenue, Baton Rouge, LA 70807.

INDEX BY INSTITUTION

University of Maryland: 317, 318, 319, 320, 321, 322, 323, 324, 325, 326, 327
University of Michigan: 348
University of Mississippi: 357
University of Missouri: 358
University of Nebraska: 503
University of Nebraska: 410
University of New Orleans: 028
University of North Carolina: 078
University of North Florida: 437, 438
University of Notre Dame: 444
University of Oklahoma: 453, 454
University of Pennsylvania: 473, 474, 475
University of Pittsburgh: 480, 481, 482
University of Portland: 484
University of San Francisco: 517
University of South Florida: 535
University of Tennessee: 556
University of Texas: 571, 572, 573, 574, 575
University of the Pacific: 469
University of Toledo: 580
University of Virginia: 606, 607, 608
University of West Florida: 616
University of Wisconsin: 633, 634, 635
Utah State University: 600
Valparaiso University: 601
Villanova University: 602
Virginia Commonwealth University: 603, 604
Virginia Union University: 605
Voorhees College: 609
W. W. Smith Foundation: 610
Warren Wilson College: 611
Washington Council for Postsecondary Education: 612
Washington Public Affairs Center: 352
Washington University: 613
Washington Urban League: 614
West Chester University: 615
West Georgia College: 617

INDEX BY DISCIPLINE

340, 342, 343, 344, 345, 346, 347, 351, 352, 354, 359, 361, 362, 363, 364, 365, 371, 372, 376, 399, 400, 407, 409, 410, 411, 412, 413, 414, 415, 422, 427, 430, 432, 433, 436, 437, 438, 439, 440, 441, 442, 444, 446, 448, 450, 452, 453, 454, 455, 457, 460, 461, 462, 463, 465, 466, 467, 468, 470, 472, 477, 479, 480, 481, 482, 483, 484, 485, 487, 489, 490, 491, 492, 493, 494, 495, 497, 499, 500, 501, 502, 503, 504, 505, 506, 507, 508, 509, 510, 511, 512, 514, 515, 516, 522, 523, 527, 528, 529, 530, 533, 534, 536, 540, 541, 543, 544, 546, 547, 548, 550, 551, 552, 553, 554, 557, 562, 565, 567, 568, 569, 570, 571, 574, 576, 578, 579, 581, 582, 583, 584, 586, 587, 588, 589, 590, 598, 599, 602, 604, 605, 606, 607, 609, 610, 611, 612, 613, 614, 615, 616, 617, 618, 621, 625, 626, 627, 630, 632, 634, 636, 639, 640, 641, 642, 645, 646, 647, 648, 649, 651

Geography: 121

Geology: 028, 029, 120, 254, 400

Government: 011, 637

Health Care: 001, 211, 246, 425

History: 119, 121, 333, 453, 524

Home Economics: 030, 031

Hotel and Restaurant Management: 496

Humanities: 119, 333, 370, 401, 453, 464, 482, 524, 620, 628, 631

Information Systems: 062

Insurance: 105, 531, 532, 577

Journalism: 012, 013, 065, 071, 072, 095, 096, 117, 160, 161, 164, 165, 177, 197, 220, 222, 275, 280, 285, 288, 304, 379, 397, 423, 426, 435, 525, 555, 564, 597, 633

Political Science: 041, 113, 121, 520

Public Relations/Affairs: 165, 519

Psychology: 042, 043, 121, 445, 498, 535, 623

Real Estate: 260

Science: 052, 120, 147, 181, 333, 358, 373, 390, 391, 394, 395, 400, 401, 431, 435, 453, 464, 535, 620, 628, 631, 643, 644

Sociology: 045, 121, 245, 358

Speech: 046, 047

Statistics: 066

Textiles: 126

Veterinary Science: 353, 425, 513

INDEX BY STATE

Ohio: 009, 051, 052, 053, 054, 055, 060, 061, 063, 082, 083, 106, 107, 123, 167, 172, 173, 287, 294, 343, 344, 345, 346, 365, 408, 451, 468, 525, 580, 630, 632, 639, 640, 641

Oklahoma: 435, 452, 453, 454

Oregon: 231, 483, 484

Pennsylvania: 003, 005, 062, 086, 087, 099, 105, 124, 180, 192, 226, 243, 244, 245, 283, 292, 295, 296, 309, 310, 312, 339, 340, 342, 354, 361, 411, 467, 472, 473, 474, 475, 480, 481, 482, 512, 540, 553, 554, 576, 602, 610, 615, 618

Rhode Island: 487

South Carolina: 126, 127, 128, 129, 130, 131, 132, 135, 150, 526, 609

South Dakota: 530

Tennessee: 188, 203, 259, 328, 335, 336, 449, 501, 556, 557, 558, 559, 589, 590, 592

Texas: 057, 073, 156, 158, 165, 189, 190, 191, 242, 249, 250, 251, 252, 253, 254, 502, 536, 560, 561, 562, 563, 564, 565, 566, 567, 568, 569, 570, 571, 572, 573, 574, 575, 582

Utah: 600

Vermont: 108

Virginia: 029, 133, 164, 193, 225, 263, 293, 311, 314, 329, 379, 430, 431, 436, 455, 456, 457, 458, 459, 460, 461, 493, 494, 495, 541, 548, 594, 595, 596, 597, 603, 604, 605, 606, 607, 608, 614

Washington: 012, 013, 612, 626, 627, 628

Washington, D.C.: see District of Columba

Wisconsin: 017, 018, 019, 020, 021, 022, 023, 024, 349, 363, 491, 492, 633, 634, 635, 636